EQUIPPED TO EVANGELIZE

A BIBLICAL FOUNDATION

ROB VENTURA

CHRISTIAN FOCUS

paperback ISBN 978-1-5271-1322-0
ebook ISBN 978-1-5271-1374-9

10 9 8 7 6 5 4 3 2 1

Published in 2025
by
Christian Focus Publications Ltd.,
Geanies House, Fearn, Ross-shire
IV20 1TW, Great Britain.

www.christianfocus.com

Cover design by Rhian Muir

Printed and bound by
Bell and Bain Glasgow

MIX
Paper | Supporting responsible forestry
FSC® C007785
www.fsc.org

Evangelism can be very difficult. When we share the gospel, we find ourselves at war with the world, our own flesh, and the spiritual forces of darkness. To equip us for the fight and to fire our hearts for this sacred duty, Rob Ventura shows why we should be motivated to share the gospel (because it brings glory to God and does good to man) and why we can be confident in doing so (because of the accompanying power of the Holy Spirit). Rob also shows that the sovereignty of God in salvation should stir up rather than quench our zeal to share the gospel with the lost. In this robust treatment of evangelism, Rob combines biblical clarity and doctrinal fidelity in a work that is sure to revive your passion for knowing Christ in the gospel and making Him known to the world.

Joel R. Beeke
Chancellor, Puritan Reformed Theological Seminary,
Grand Rapids, Michigan

This is an excellent primer on evangelism, written by a pastor with a shepherd's heart. I appreciate the strong emphasis on being biblical in our approach to evangelism, especially given the damage caused by man-centered methods. This is exactly the kind of book I am eager to place in the hands of all our members. Personally, I often need a book like this to reignite my own passion for reaching the lost. Rob Ventura has masterfully distilled the full scope of evangelism into a succinct and impactful guide. I am delighted to recommend it.

Conrad Mbewe
Pastor, Kabwata Baptist Church,
Lusaka, Zambia

A concise work on evangelism that is chock-full of biblical truth. It encompasses all that the Christian and the church need to know to go forth and preach the gospel. It is both instructional and motivational. It can be read and studied alone by a believer or taught in a classroom setting in a church or institute. In the realm of evangelistic literature, this work is in the sweet spot—not too much, not too little.

Paul Washer
Founder and Director, HeartCry Missionary Society

Rob Ventura's new book on evangelism is an uncomfortable read. It is refreshingly biblical, but it is also searchingly pointed. Rob's aim is not to leave his readers informed, but to spur them to action. The chapters are brief, engaging, and rounded off with four questions to drive home the teaching. If every gospel church gave all its members this book, who knows what God might do!

Ian Hamilton
Professor of Historical Theology, Westminster Seminary, Newcastle

All of us need to take seriously the call to engage in the work of evangelism. We also need sound biblical teaching on this subject. This helpful new book provides exactly that. This work is a powerful resource that will equip and prompt you to action for the great task of proclaiming the good news of Christ to sinners. Pick it up, read it, and put it into practice.

Jonathan Master
President, Greenville Presbyterian Theological Seminary, Greenville, South Carolina

I'm thrilled to see such a thoughtful book on evangelism so well anchored in Scripture. For decades, Western Christianity has approached evangelism based on purely pragmatic principles—sometimes even scorning doctrinal precision or dismissing "too much Scripture" as a hindrance to soul winning. But the gospel, as Scripture explains, is the power of God for salvation. We cannot abbreviate, soften, alter, or add to the message and think we are doing proper evangelism. Rob Ventura understands this, and he knows what a priority evangelism should be in the heart of every Christian. This excellent book will both motivate and encourage you with a truly biblical strategy for winning people to Christ. I highly recommend it.

Phil Johnson
Executive Director, Grace to You Ministries,
Sun Valley, California

Wow! What a great book on evangelism! Written in an engaging and accessible style, it is both pointed and practical. Theologically sound, it corrects many wrong or imbalanced ideas about evangelism. Without being overly polemical, it focuses mainly on the positive explanation and application of the Bible's teaching on this subject. It has a pastoral flavor, helpful anecdotes, quotes and illustrations, and urgent appeals that bring both conviction and heart-stirring motivation. I will be promoting this book to my own congregation.

Jeffery Smith
Pastor, Emmanuel Baptist Church,
Coconut Creek, Florida

Rob's new book on evangelism is a stirring call to scatter gospel seeds far and wide. Rooted in an unshakable biblical authority, it echoes the wisdom of legendary voices like Edwards, Whitefield, Spurgeon, and others. This book will ignite your passion for reaching the lost. Get it!

Mark Chanski
Coordinator, Reformed Baptist Network

Contents

of its success, the Christian comes to think it's not worth it to even try, believing that his or her efforts have been wasted if no one was converted. This is why, for example, I would reject definitions such as those put forth by "Church Growth" advocate Peter Wagner, who says "Evangelism has only been accomplished when disciples are made."[1] Darius Salter is another who defines evangelism in terms of success, stating that our definition must leave room "for the evaluation of effectiveness."[2]

Such definitions are odd to me, considering that conversion is one of the most challenging areas of all Christianity to evaluate. Even Christ implies this in parables such as the "Parable of the Sower," where what looks like genuine evidence of conversion proves to be counterfeit (Mark 4:1-20). While we certainly can evaluate people's fruits to see if they are in a state of grace, ultimately, only God knows whether a person has been truly converted, so how can we limit evangelism to what is known to produce converts? Such thinking led Charles Spurgeon to deep lamentation: "What mean these dispatches from the battlefield? 'Last night 14 souls were under conviction, 15 were justified, and 8 received full sanctification.' I am weary of these public braggings, this counting of unhatched chickens, this exhibition of doubtful spoils. Lay aside such numberings of the people, such idle pretense of certifying in half a minute that which will need the testing of a lifetime."[3]

---

1 C. Peter Wagner, *Church Growth and the Whole Gospel* (San Francisco: Harper & Row, 1981), 56.

2 Darius Salter, *American Evangelism* (Grand Rapids: Baker Book House, 1996), 22-23.

3 As quoted in Iain H. Murray, *Revival & Revivalism* (Carlisle: The Banner of Truth Trust, 1994), 408.

But thankfully, such definitions of *evangelism* are not our only option. There is another way, and one that is biblical. The word "evangelism" comes from a Greek verb that means "to declare, bring, or preach good news." Thus, at its core, to evangelize simply means "to proclaim good news."[4]

In the Bible, its meaning is more narrowly focused on "telling or sharing the good news or the gospel of Jesus Christ with others."[5] That's it! Biblical evangelism is that straightforward. When we are evangelizing, we are "gospeling,"[6] which is to say we are spreading the message about Jesus, the Savior.

Such a definition as this should help recalibrate how we see the practice of evangelism since evangelism happens even if people aren't saved. It is no longer about whether we can force or manipulate someone into believing what we share with them. Instead, we joyfully leave the results to God, knowing that "Salvation is of the Lord" (Jonah 2:9). Success in evangelism is not about numbers *but faithfulness*

---

4 I will open up the major components of this good news in greater detail in chapter five.

5 It should be noted that I believe evangelism can assume many forms, as I discuss throughout this book, such as personal witnessing in a one-on-one work setting, a restaurant, parents evangelizing their children at home, tract distribution, standing on a soapbox in the public square, going door-to-door, or both home and foreign missions. Additionally, my definition should show that there is a difference between giving one's testimony and evangelism. While sharing one's testimony is a good thing, and often leads to evangelism, there is a distinction between the two. Testifying to what God has done in our lives bears witness to what Jesus has done for us. However, it does not by itself give the content of the gospel which is Christ Himself. Additionally, living a holy life before others is crucial, but it alone is not evangelism. Such a life testifies to the power of the gospel, but it does not tell others about the gospel.

6 "What is Evangelism?" *Ligonier*, https://www.ligonier.org/learn/devotionals/what-evangelism (last accessed Jan. 28, 2025).

to share the gospel message. It is about delivering and announcing—not converting. J. I. Packer agrees, saying that "if we regard our job, not simply to present Christ, but actually to produce converts…our approach to evangelism would become pragmatic and calculating. Techniques would become ends in themselves."[7] For Packer, evangelism is not about conversions, but about "whether you are faithfully making known the gospel message."[8] In fact, in answering the question of how evangelism should be defined, Packer says "The New Testament answer is very simple. According to the New Testament, evangelism is just preaching the gospel, the evangel. It is a work of communication in which Christians make themselves mouthpieces for God's message of mercy to sinners."[9]

This, of course, is not to say that we aren't eager to see souls saved. Heaven rejoices at the salvation of one repentant sinner, and we do as well (Luke 15:10). It also doesn't mean we do not earnestly entreat people to repent and believe when we evangelize. Like Paul, our aim when evangelizing should be to plead with others to be reconciled to God (2 Cor. 5:20). We must fervently pray and weep for souls. But it is up to God to give spiritual life. We can beseech and weep, but unless God moves on the person who hears the gospel and opens their heart (Acts 16:14), nothing will happen. *Faithfulness in sharing the gospel is our job, not producing numbers.*

Popular writer Donald Whitney agrees. In writing about our topic, he asked,

---

7 J.I. Packer, *Evangelism and the Sovereignty of God* (Downers Grove: Intervarsity Press, 1961), 122.

8 Packer, *Evangelism,* 41.

9 Packer, *Evangelism,* 41.

> What is success in evangelism? Is it when the person you witness to comes to Christ? Certainly that's what we want to happen. But if this is success, are we failures whenever we share the gospel and people refuse to believe? Was Jesus an "evangelistic failure" when people like the rich young ruler turned away from Him and His message? Obviously not. Then neither are we when we present Christ and His message and they turn away in unbelief. We need to learn that sharing the gospel *is* successful evangelism. We ought to have an obsession for souls, and tearful pleading with God to see more people converted, but conversions are the fruit that God alone can give.[10]

Doesn't such a view of evangelism free up the reader to want to share the gospel? Doesn't it motivate you to be involved in this most sacred task? Isn't it liberating to know that the only failure in evangelism is not doing it? If you have faithfully shared the gospel according to God's Word, then you were successful. You were faithful to the call to evangelize your neighbor, who, biblically speaking, is anyone near you. Hence, the reason why our biblical definition is so crucial.

Why Is Evangelism Necessary?

This leads us back to where we began our discussion at the start of the chapter. Biblical evangelism is critical at any time, but this is especially true today in the period and culture in which we live. There is a great need for evangelism because the gospel is the only lasting, eternal remedy for the lost.

As we consider the need for evangelism, we should note that our society is similar to the one that Paul addressed in his letter to the Romans. Pagans, unbelievers, and fornicators

10 Donald S. Whitney, *Spiritual Disciplines for the Christian Life* (Colorado Springs: NavPress, 1991), 103.

lived side by side with very religious Jews, and they were all lost and heading to hell. This is what we find in the world. There are very religious people among us, but much of their religion is nominal. At the same time there is much non-religious activity that occupies the attention of many, such as the idolatrous worship of sports and entertainment, along with an increase in occultic practices. If we can see how Paul approached such a situation with a view to seeing sinners made right with God through Jesus, we can apply it to our context. So what was Paul's remedy for people in the messy and godless Roman Empire? What did he see as the biblical solution?

First, the apostle reminds us that all people are guilty before God and under His just condemnation: "For the wrath of God is revealed from heaven against all ungodliness and unrighteousness of men, who suppress the truth in unrighteousness" (Rom. 1:18). Notice that it is the "ungodliness and unrighteousness of men" that provokes God's just anger. The human being is the one at fault, *not God*. This is partly because all people have been given insight into the reality of God's existence. They know certain of His attributes and are thus "without excuse" or, more literally, without legal defense (Rom. 1:20).[11] The person's conscience, as well as God's creation, testifies to God's existence, righteousness, and eternal power, but people have suppressed it. They have lived without gratitude or thankfulness to Him (Rom. 1:21). They have become "futile in their thoughts, and their foolish

11 Here, the apostle is acting as a prosecuting attorney. He is saying that unbelievers are without a valid reason for the rejection of God since general revelation about Him is so effective. Clearly, then, he's teaching us that the problem with humanity is not that they lack the knowledge that there is one true and living God. Rather, he says that they will not respond correctly to it.

hearts were darkened" (Rom. 1:21). They became worshipers of idols and of themselves, serving "the creature rather than the Creator, who is blessed forever. Amen" (Rom. 1:23, 25).

Such a picture of the Roman Empire reads like a description of any society where godlessness reigns, including our own. Perversity, drugs, violence, spiritism, and false religion are rampant today, as was the case in Paul's context. Consider the description of the evils which conclude Romans 1:

> And even as they did not like to retain God in their knowledge, God gave them over to a debased mind, to do those things which are not fitting; being filled with all unrighteousness, sexual immorality, wickedness, covetousness, maliciousness; full of envy, murder, strife, deceit, evil-mindedness; they are whisperers, backbiters, haters of God, violent, proud, boasters, inventors of evil things, disobedient to parents, undiscerning, untrustworthy, unloving, unforgiving, unmerciful; who, knowing the righteous judgment of God, that those who practice such things are deserving of death, not only do the same but also approve of those who practice them (Rom. 1:28-32).[12]

Second, Paul reminds us that there's another sector of society that isn't into sexual deviancy or paganism but still desperately needs the Savior. He addresses such people in Romans 2. These are the people who are outraged by violence and drugs, yet they approach it from an angle of self-righteous disinterest. These are the cults, formalists, and religious Pharisees. They are trying to get to heaven

12 For an exposition of these words, or any other words found in this book from the book of Romans, the reader can consider my commentary on Romans: *Expository Outlines and Observations on Romans, Hints and Helps for Preachers and Teachers* (Fearn, UK: Mentor, 2023), 93-94.

based on their own merit or worth. They fast twice a week, give alms to the poor (Luke 18:12), and often look at sinners all around them with haughty disapproval. These are zealous Roman Catholics, Mormons, Jehovah's Witnesses, or, tragically, even some people in the professing Christian church. This is a type of dead orthodoxy or false religion; it is outward religion without inward regeneration of the heart. They think their religion, tradition, and rituals can save them. Not so, says Paul. Such folks are in no better condition than the sinners they look down upon. In Romans 3:10-18, Paul then summarizes the situation concerning all people, whether religious or not:

> There is none righteous, no, not one;
> There is none who understands;
> There is none who seeks after God.
> They have all turned aside;
> They have together become unprofitable;
> There is none who does good, no, not one.
> Their throat is an open tomb;
> With their tongues they have practiced deceit;
> The poison of asps is under their lips;
> Whose mouth is full of cursing and bitterness.
> Their feet are swift to shed blood;
> Destruction and misery are in their ways;
> And the way of peace they have not known.
> There is no fear of God before their eyes.

Having written this, thankfully, Paul doesn't leave us without hope. He doesn't simply describe the scene and then throw up his hands in great despair and grim pessimism. Rather, he tells us that the remedy is the gospel, and so, even though "all have sinned and fall short of the glory of God," such fallen sinners through the gospel can be "justified freely by

His grace through the redemption that is in Christ Jesus" (Rom. 3:23-24). This is what Paul calls "the power of God to salvation for everyone who believes" (Rom. 1:16). Such a gospel is full, wide, and free to all (I will speak about this more in the next chapter). It is for Jew or Gentile, pagan or self-righteous Pharisee. This is why he told us back in Romans 1 that he is "not ashamed"[13] or embarrassed about the gospel of Christ (Rom. 1:16). And why should he be since the gospel is the instrument through which the saving power of God operates in order to rescue men and women from their sins (1 Cor. 1:18)? It is the plain preaching of the gospel that is the means through which God's omnipotence works to bring spiritually dead sinners to new life in His Son. As the great Puritan William Gurnall said, the gospel is "the chariot wherein the spirit rides victoriously when he makes his entrance into the hearts of men." This is why the gospel is the only message worth proclaiming. This is why Paul was not ashamed of it.

But this leads to a new problem. Now that we know the gospel is the great remedy for lost souls, how will it spread? How can people actually be saved by it? Does God just zap people in their sleep? Does He write out the gospel for them on tree leaves or in the clouds of the sky? Does He send Michael or Gabriel down to herald the good news? Again, Paul doesn't leave us guessing. He tells us exactly how this gospel is to be spread.

---

13 The word ashamed here in the Greek text is a present tense verb indicating habitual disposition. The point is, Paul was not at all ashamed of the gospel, nor would he ever be—the gospel, which was centered on the doing, the dying, and the rising of Jesus Christ our Lord on our behalf.

The Four-Fold Call to Evangelize

It won't surprise anyone to hear that the Apostle Paul was the model evangelist, aside from Jesus Christ Himself. Paul doesn't merely emphasize the importance of speaking to the lost about Jesus, which is true enough, but he says his life's work is to do so (1 Cor. 9:17-22). Even as he gives us the marvelous predestinarian passages of Romans 9 and Ephesians 1, he also sees himself as having a vital part to play when it comes to the saving of souls.[14] What is more, he wants to make sure nothing hinders him from this: "I have made myself a servant to all, that I may win more" (1 Cor. 9:19). He tells us that he wants to "win Jews" (1 Cor. 9:20). He also wants to win "the weak" (1 Cor. 9:22). Paul was thoroughly convinced that he was a conduit through which people were won to God (1 Cor. 3:5). He even tells us that he seeks to win souls in any or every way, or by "all means" (1 Cor. 9:22).

Such a background into Paul's mindset helps us to understand better what is meant by his four-fold "how" call to evangelize when he writes in Romans 10:14-15a: "*How* then shall they call on Him in whom they have not believed?[15] And *how* shall they believe in Him of whom

14 This highlights an important point: biblical Calvinism is no hindrance to biblical evangelism. The biblical doctrine of election was no deterrent for Paul's widespread evangelizing. In fact, it was the very impetus for it—more on this in chapter two.

15 In Greek, the verbs in verses 14 and 15 are in the subjunctive mood. The subjunctive mood is the mood of potentiality—of whether or not something will or could happen. In our passage, the answers are all assumed to be negative so that people could not do what is being asked in the questions. Paul here is not speaking absolutely, but relatively; hence, for example, this does not negate the fact that many people are saved just by simply reading the Word of God and not by hearing a preacher. However, in either case (the hearing or the reading of the Word) is necessary (cf. James 1:18; 1 Pet. 1:22-25).

they have not heard? And *how* shall they hear without a preacher? And *how* shall they preach unless they are sent?" Here Paul tells us that people have to call on Christ in order to be saved for "whoever calls on the name of the Lord shall be saved" (Rom. 10:13). This is the idea of laying hold of and believing in Christ alone for salvation. "For by grace you have been saved through faith" (Eph. 2:8). But true faith expresses itself by calling on Christ. The point is, you don't call on someone you don't believe in, and you certainly can't call on someone you've never heard of. But "how shall they hear without a preacher?" And "how shall they preach unless they are sent?"[16] The answer to these questions is: they cannot. This is the crucial part that evangelism plays, and specifically, the part of human agency in connection to it (as I will expound more in chapter four). God uses means to convert people. The means God uses is that of us sharing the gospel with others so that they might hear its truth.

We see this, for example, in Paul's letters, where an emphasis on "hearing" is found in many. Writing to the Romans, Paul says, "So then faith comes *by hearing*, and hearing by the word of God" (Rom. 10:17). When writing to the Thessalonians, he says, "For this reason we also thank God without ceasing, because when you received the word of God *which you heard from us*, you welcomed it not as the word of men, but as it is in truth, the word of God, which also effectively works in you who believe" (1 Thess. 2:13). Again, when writing to the Galatians, Paul says, "Did you receive the Spirit by the works of the Law, or by *hearing with faith?*" (Gal. 3:2). And to the Ephesians he says, "In Him you also trusted, after you *heard the word of truth*, the gospel

16 Generally speaking, I understand that this sending is done through a local church (cf. Acts 13:1-3).

of your salvation" (Eph. 1:13). Hearing requires someone speaking. It presupposes that a human being will make contact with another human being and share the message of life with them, which is found in Christ.

Thus, Christians must be involved in evangelism because this is God's way of spreading the gospel, which is the great remedy for lost souls. This is God's means of them hearing about Jesus, the only Savior of sinners.

For Reflection and Discussion

- What is the definition of biblical evangelism?
- What are some wrong methods of evangelism and why?
- Why is it essential for us to be involved in evangelism?
- In what ways can you be involved in it?

2

The Scope of Biblical Evangelism

We cannot bring the whole world to Christ, but we must bring Christ to the whole world.

—John Blanchard

Who is to be the focus of our evangelistic efforts? Who are the targets of our evangelism? These are the questions before us in this chapter, and while the answer is simple, acting on the answer is more challenging than it may seem. The Bible teaches that the scope of our evangelism is to be all people everywhere, without distinction (Matt. 28:19-20). However, how often do we find ourselves making distinctions when it comes to our evangelistic efforts? How often do our personal biases or resentments keep us from sharing the gospel with everyone?

For example, most Christians today would readily admit that the gospel should go to everyone. Whether Jew or Gentile, male or female, plumber or professor, all are within the gospel's scope. People in China and India need to be evangelized just as much as persons in New York City or London. The same is true about our neighbors, coworkers, and extended family. And yet, functionally, this isn't always how things play out.

For instance, in a time like ours, when polarization seems to be at its peak, it is easy to exclude our enemies from the scope of the gospel. It is easy to regard liberals, homosexuals, or abortionists as our enemies rather than as potential recipients of God's amazing grace. This isn't to excuse such people's sins, nor is it to deny that such lifestyles are hostile to God and His people. It is to say, rather, that political, sexual, and ethnical barriers can often blind us to the fact that no one, including those whom we perceive to be the worst of sinners, are outside the reach of the gospel (1 Tim. 1:15-16). Sadly, at times, our prejudices can cause us to be like Jonah, who was so outraged by the prospect of God's grace being extended to the pagans in Nineveh that he immediately jumped on a ship and headed in the opposite direction to where God had called him to speak.

As we approach the subject of our chapter, each of us must ask ourselves some hard and honest questions. Who are certain "enemies" that we struggle to see as potential recipients of grace? Which people would we have a hard time sharing the gospel with? Could it be the LGBTQ+ people, Muslims, Catholics, Deb from accounting, your mother-in-law, father-in-law, or the bully from high school who always stole your snacks? How would you feel about pedophiles in prison or rapists on the streets hearing the gospel and getting saved by it? You get the point. It's easy to build high walls of resentment that keep us from sharing the good news of Jesus Christ effectively and earnestly with certain people. It is easy to see such people as unworthy of our gospel labors. Such attitudes often reveal our lack of love for sinners. Consequently, Spurgeon was right when he said, "a soul winner must first be a soul lover."[1]

This is why it is essential to drill down on what it means for our evangelism's "scope" to be all people everywhere, without distinction. It is easy to say that we believe this in the abstract, but it is typically much harder to apply. From the Bible's perspective, it is obvious who is within the gospel's scope—it is everyone! However, because of our indwelling sin, resentment, pride, and the realities of life, the Bible's perspective is not always what we adopt. Thus, a fresh understanding of our topic is imperative for us.

Sectarianism in the Early Church

Even the early church needed a kick in the pants when it came to the scope of evangelism. On the Day of Pentecost, 3,000 souls were wonderfully added to the local church in Jerusalem (Acts 2:41). These were exciting times. There was great power and unity of mind among the believers. They were devoting themselves to "the apostle's doctrine and fellowship, in the breaking of bread, and in prayers" (Acts 2:42). They were meeting together regularly in the Temple, as well as house to house (Acts 2:46). Miracles were being wrought in their midst through the apostles' hands and even by their shadows (Acts 5:12, 15). The gospel was being preached with unction in the face of resistance and jailing (Acts 5:7-42). And yet, for all that, there weren't any Gentiles in their ranks (Acts 6:1).[2]

---

1 C.H. Spurgeon, *The Salt Cellars, Volume 1: Being a Collection of Proverbs, Together with Homily Notes Thereon* (Bellingham: Faithlife, 2009).

2 I realize that from Acts 8:4 forward, we have the mission of the Gentiles beginning with Phillip's ministry to the Samaritans, the conversion of the Ethiopian eunuch, and Peter's ministry to Aeneas in

Not yet. What is more, no one seemed to see this as a problem. No one, that is, *except God.*

How do we know that no Gentiles had officially been added to the church's number yet, at least in terms of formal connection? The answer is because of the Apostles' shock when it finally happens. Before we get there, let's look at how it comes about. First, we have a Roman soldier named Cornelius who comes on the scene around ten years after Pentecost (Acts 10:1). We are told that he was "a devout man and one who feared God with all his household, who gave alms generously to the people, and prayed to God always" (Acts 10:2). This means that he was broadly connected to the Jewish religion being a pious man, but he's by no means considered a full-fledged Jew.[3] He's still a Gentile. He's considered unclean by the Jews. This is why the Apostles will be outraged when they find out Peter went to this man's house and ate with him (Acts 11:3). Note that point well. Initially, the apostles themselves had a difficult time appreciating that the scope of the gospel was more expansive than being just for the Jewish people. More on that in a moment. Before they can appreciate that fact, God must intervene in an unusual way. Their narrowness must be expanded. But how does it happen?

Cornelius receives a vision of an angel of God who tells him to send men to Peter, who is staying in a nearby town by the sea (Acts 10:4-8). But such a one-sided vision wouldn't

---

Acts chapter 9 (who presumably was a Gentile living in Lydda, a coastal plain about 22 miles northwest of Jerusalem). Some scholars speculate that this particular ministry of Peter was preparatory concerning what God would teach him more fully with reference to Cornelius and the Gentiles as a people in Acts 10.

3 For further explanation of this see, Eckhard E. Schnabel, *Exegetical Commentary on the New Testament* (Grand Rapids: Zondervan, 2012), 494.

be enough. The Jewish prejudice against Gentiles was so entrenched that Peter also needed a similar revelation. God gives him one while he is on the roof praying. Peter sees a cloth coming down with unclean animals on it. A voice from heaven tells him, "Rise, Peter; kill and eat" (Acts 10:13). At first, Peter rejects the vision, saying he's never eaten anything unclean before. God speaks to him a second, and then a third time (Acts 10:15-16). Peter is mystified by it all, but while he is pondering the vision, he hears the men from Cornelius down below. They are there to bring him to Cornelius's house. Peter begins to realize the meaning of the vision—Gentiles are not to be considered "unclean" as was customarily believed and taught, for God had "cleansed" them (Acts 10:15).

Peter would never have gone with the messengers had God not intervened in such a marvelous way. The same is true for us. In our natural state, we all have people who we see as unclean, common, and enemies. For blue-collar folks, this could be white-collar politicians or academics. For white-collar folks, this could be electricians or janitors. Both groups may see each other as different and strange. They don't see "eye to eye" on most things. Perhaps this is a neighbor who has rainbow flags and yard signs with godless politicians on them. These are a few examples out of a thousand. The point is, we all have these prejudices against certain people or people groups. This dramatically affects our evangelism because we become reluctant to pray for such individuals, much less share the gospel with them. We often feel that they are unworthy of our time or effort, so we don't try. Therefore, we need God's grace to work a change in us, as was done for Peter. We need God's Word to show us that all people outside of Christ are lost, therefore they desperately need to be evangelized by us.

Now that Peter has been shown this truth by God, he doesn't hesitate to go along with Cornelius's messengers, even though hours before he would have refused. When Peter arrives at Cornelius's house, still not exactly sure what is going on, he is told by Cornelius that he is supposed to tell them all the things that God commanded him (Acts 10:33). What Peter does next is what is described in the first chapter as evangelism. Peter is called on to share the Savior with these Gentiles. After he does so, we are told that "the Holy Spirit fell upon all those who heard the word" (Acts 10:44). What was Peter's response and the response of the Jews who had come with him? Astonishment and shock. Why? "Because the gift of the Holy Spirit had been poured out *on the Gentiles also*." The salvation of Cornelius and his household showed that God Himself deemed them just as fitting of the gospel as the Jews were (Acts 10:45).

Today we take it for granted that God saves Gentiles, or non-Jewish people. This isn't as shocking as it was for Peter and the early church. But do we not still experience such shock and even outrage when specific people are converted, to our shame? What would happen if the homosexual neighbor across the street got radically saved? How do people react upon hearing someone like serial killer Jeffrey Dahmer just might be in heaven now? What about atheists who go looking to find ways to discredit Christianity but then get saved in the process? What about the hecklers in George Whitefield's day who came to the meetings to throw cats at him but then were saved through his preaching? What about the missionaries to China who talk about Communists getting converted after years of persecuting

Christians? Yes, there are great enemies of God in the world, but these same enemies still fall within the gospel's scope. They all need to be evangelized. The Wiccans, pagans, and your boss all need to hear about Jesus.

To the Apostles' credit, after Peter returns to Jerusalem and reports what God has done among the Gentiles, they "glorify God, saying, 'Then God has also granted to the Gentiles repentance to life'" (Acts 11:18). These men were no Jonah, although in a sense they had some reason to be, for Roman soldiers such as Cornelius were seen as great enemies of the Jewish people. Cornelius wasn't merely a Gentile, he was a mercenary of Caesar. He had one of the most offensive occupations a person could have in Judea. But God was showing the Apostles that the scope of the gospel was for Jews and Gentiles, *even the worst of them.* The Christians outside of Jerusalem were also learning this lesson, for we are told that originally those who had been scattered because of the persecution in Jerusalem preached the word "*to no one but Jews only*" (Acts 11:19). However, Paul's later international missionary endeavors would help remove such prejudices, though it wasn't without controversy (Acts 15:1-21).

Nothing New

Among the early church, such skepticism regarding the scope of the gospel was inexcusable in light of the Old Testament. The idea of the gospel being for all the world, not just for Jews, was not a new idea. The gospel itself can be traced back to the Garden of Eden (Gen. 3:15). In the first gospel promise found in the Bible, generally known as the *protoevangelium*, God tells the serpent that the Seed of the woman will one day "bruise your head [a fatal blow], and you shall bruise His heel [an injury, but not permanent]". This language refers to the victorious, substitutionary death that Jesus Christ, the Son of God, would eventually endure for sinners on the cross. Such a promise as this is given before there is any Jewish/Gentile distinction. Therefore, just as the call "to be fruitful and multiply; fill the earth and subdue it" is universal in scope, so also is the promise of the gospel.

Additionally, even before Christ came into the world, the prophets spoke about Him as being a "light for all the nations" (Isa. 42:6) and as the one who would bring salvation "to the ends of the earth" (Isa. 49:6). We are also told that He would be a "light to bring revelation to the Gentiles" (Luke 2:32).[4]

This universal nature of the gospel is even further seen in God's promise to Abraham. God takes Abram (before his name changes to Abraham) and declares that He will make him "a great nation" and that his name will be "great," and that in Abraham "all the families of the earth shall be blessed" (Gen. 12:1-3). Such a promise as this must have seemed extraordinary to Abram. He was just an ordinary man. His means, though prosperous, were nothing compared to others in his day. He was no Pharaoh. This was a private man of wealth and some local power, but not much beyond that. Not when he was first starting out. More importantly, his wife Sarah was past childbearing years. The idea of this man becoming a great nation or a blessing to all the families of the earth would have been inconceivable for him. And yet, note the scope of this promise. The blessing to Abraham

4 Of course, it should be noted that throughout the Gospels, Jesus ministered to Gentiles (Matt. 15:21-31; Mark 5:1-29, 7:24-30; John 4). All of this gives us indications of His love for all humanity.

is not for his family only. The scope is "all the families of the earth." Thus, this would not merely be a "nation of Israel" thing. And how do we know that? The answer is because Paul tells us so.

In Galatians 3:8, Paul says, "the Scripture, foreseeing that God would justify *the Gentiles by faith, preached the gospel to Abraham beforehand*." Now if this was all the information that Paul gave us about this passage, it would leave us guessing where and how the gospel was preached to Abraham. But Paul doesn't leave us guessing. He says the gospel was preached to Abraham when God told him, "In you all the nations shall be blessed" (Gal. 3:8). But how is this a gospel proclamation? The gospel proclamation is in the good news of what God was ultimately going to accomplish through the Redeemer, Jesus, who is "the seed" of Abraham in whom all the nations of the earth are blessed (Gen. 22:18). In Genesis 22:18, God does not say to Abraham that the blessing of all the nations is in his "seeds" as of many, no, but as of one, "'And to your Seed,' who is Christ" (Gal. 3:16).

Returning to the main point: Abraham's offspring are not limited to ethnic Jews but include anyone who believes in Christ. Consequently, Paul declares in Galatians 3:29, "And if you are Christ's, then you are Abraham's seed, and heirs according to the promise."

Now we can make sense of God's promise to Abraham when He takes him outside to look at the stars: "And He brought him outside and said, 'Look toward heaven, and number the stars, if you are able to count them.' Then He said to him, 'So shall your offspring be!'" (Gen. 15:5). Is God here promising Abraham a plethora of physical seed? In a sense, yes. But that is not the whole picture. Abraham's physical offspring would be abundant. All the tribes of Israel would come from his loins. But there is something more important going on here. As we interpret "Scripture with Scripture," we learn that Abraham has spiritual offspring, and again, this refers to those who are in Christ, whether they are physical descendants of Abraham or not. This is why Paul says elsewhere, "he is not a Jew who is one outwardly, nor is circumcision that which is outward in the flesh. But he is a Jew who is one inwardly; and circumcision is that which is of the heart, by the Spirit" (Rom. 2:28-29). Additionally, we're told in Romans 9:25-26, "I will call them 'My people', who were not 'My people', and her 'beloved' who was not beloved. And it shall come to pass in the place where it was said to them, 'You are not My people' there they shall be called sons of the living God."

These are remarkable statements concerning God's promise to Abraham's spiritual seed. Whether we are Jews or Gentiles, if we have saving faith in Christ, we are children of Abraham and children of God. More importantly for us, the key to God's multiethnic promise is in the fact that His people, throughout the world, regardless of their background, will be saved through hearing the gospel, "the word of truth" (James 1:18). This means that the scope of the gospel must be universal, or to all the nations. Thus, our evangelism must have this aim as well.

This was also Jesus' message to Nicodemus. Jesus' statement to him that "God so loved the world" (John 3:16) comes on the heels of a centuries-old debate within Jewish circles. For whom is salvation? Who are God's people? Is salvation for Abraham's physical descendants only, or is it also for the nations? In Jesus' day, the non-Jewish nations were seen as filthy and barbaric to the Jews. Even Gentiles who converted to Judaism were not allowed full access to the Temple, which is one of the reasons Jesus cleansed it, teaching that God's house "shall be called a house of prayer *for all nations*" (Mark 11:17). Gentile converts such as Cornelius were to be put to death if they passed beyond the "Court of the Gentiles." This is what makes Jesus' claim in John 3 so bewildering to a man like Nicodemus. God sent Jesus into the world, not for Jews only but also for Gentiles, or "the world" (John 3:16). Hence, "For God so loved *the world* that He gave His only begotten Son" means vastly more than what Nicodemus and other Jews at the time were expecting. The "whosoever believes" part of the verse would have been just as baffling since Jesus is now saying that even if a pagan believes in Him, he is just as much a child of God with full incorporation into God's spiritual family as any physical, believing descendent of Abraham would be.

Matthew 28 and the Great Commission

The gospel's wide-reaching scope can especially be seen in the "Great Commission" passages of the Gospels, and specifically in Matthew 28:18-20:

> And Jesus came and spoke to them, saying, "All authority has been given to Me in heaven and on earth. Go therefore and make disciples of all the nations, baptizing them in the name of the Father and of the Son and of the Holy Spirit, teaching them to observe all things that I have commanded you; and lo, I am with you always, even to the end of the age."

Most readers will readily admit that Jesus is speaking here of worldwide evangelism to be taken up by Christians in every age. However, such an understanding of the passage was not always so obvious. In fact, in the eighteenth century, the Northamptonshire Baptist Association of England met to discuss the meaning of this passage and whether it commanded that the gospel should be taken to the lost all over the world or not. The future father of modern missions, William Carey, was at that meeting. He suggested that Matthew 28 clearly commanded us to take the gospel to the nations, for he questioned how it could go to all the world apart from human instrumentality. John Collett Ryland, pastor of a nearby church, rebuked Carey, saying, "You are a miserable enthusiast for asking such a question … What, Sir! Can you preach in Arabic, in Persian, in Hindustani, in Bengali, that you think it your duty to send the gospel to the heathens?" He then followed with perhaps the most regrettable rebuke in church history: "Young man, sit down. When God pleases to convert the heathen, he will do it without your aid or mine."[5] For Ryland and others, this passage in Matthew's gospel was only for the Apostles. It was not to extend to the generations following them. But is this accurate? And just as importantly, what are the implications of holding to such a view?

First, consider Jesus' authority. Having just been gloriously raised from the dead as He said He would be (Matt. 17:22-23), our Lord announces that He has "all authority," and that it is something that has been "given" to Him by His Father above. This authority is not localized or narrow. It is expansive and universal in scope. It is "in heaven and on earth." Thus, here is our Lord Jesus Christ. He's just defeated sin, death, and the grave. He's the royal and regal king of the world, and what is one of the first things He does? He makes the solemn pronouncement that absolute rule has been given to Him. Therefore, the disciples are to act!

---

5 As quoted in Michael Haykin, "Hyper-Calvinism and the Theology of John Gill," *Credo Magazine* (Sep. 2019).

Second, consider Jesus' assignment. He says, by way of a command, that His disciples are to "Go therefore and make disciples of all the nations." They are to baptize saved people in the name of the Father and the Son and of the Holy Spirit and teach them to observe all the things that He commanded.[6] This was the reason for proclaiming His cosmic rule at that exact juncture in history. He was about to give a worldwide task to His followers that would be utterly absurd and impossible if it wasn't for this supremacy over all things. The point is His universal Lordship *means a universal mission.*

But it is this idea of "all of the nations" that is important for us as we consider the scope of our evangelism. Jesus doesn't merely say here that we are to go to some of the nations. He doesn't say that we are just to go to the Jewish nations and make disciples, as some of His hearers would have been expecting. But what does He say? He says that because all authority in heaven and on earth has been given to Him, we must therefore go and make disciples of all the peoples. Because He is ruler over all, all people on the face of the earth are to hear about Him. Wherever there are people, the glorious message of Christ is to be proclaimed, regardless of background, ethnicity, occupation, or culture. This is the scope of our evangelistic efforts. Jesus' words plainly point to the global character of the gospel summons. Differences in culture, race, temperament, and location are to be no obstruction to what our Lord has commanded.

Shortly after this, He says once again that His disciples were to be His witnesses "in Jerusalem, and in all Judea and Samaria, *and to the end of the earth*" (Acts 1:8). Do you see

6 Ultimately, this teaching was to continue in the local church as the book of Acts clearly shows (Acts 2:42).

how wide His heart is for all people? Can you catch how broad His aim is concerning the church's mission?

But do we still have this command given to us today? Are the nations still needing to be discipled, taught, and baptized? Are there still people who need the saving work of Christ applied to their souls? Of course! This is why this "Great Commission" from Jesus still applies today, even until "the end of the age." This is the reason we continue to send out missionaries. And this is the reason we continue to plant churches in difficult places. Although Christ spoke these words to the disciples who were in front of him, it would have been impossible for them to fulfill this command in their lifetime all by themselves.

Third, consider Jesus' assurance. This is the reason why He ends this charge by saying, "Lo, I[7] am with you always." Here, Jesus means to show us that it's not only the first-century disciples who have been assigned this great task of worldwide evangelism. It is likewise given to every disciple who would come after them as well. He is saying by way of encouragement that as we go out and do the work of evangelism to all people even in our day, He Himself will be with us always, just as He was with the early church, even to the consummation of the age.

Consider this from another angle. Here our Lord tells the disciples to make, baptize, and teach other disciples to obey all the things that he had commanded them, as we read above. Well, part of that teaching would include these Great Commission words to evangelize all as recorded here. Our Lord says that disciples are to make other disciples, and they, in turn, were to teach others to do so as well.

---

7 Or more literally from the Greek text: "I, even I am" or "I myself am," stressing the surety of the matter.

Therefore, these Great Commission words are just as much in force for us today as when our Lord spoke them to this small group of followers. Here, Jesus is commanding the disciples to carry the gospel into all the lands and to not quit in this work until all the nations have embraced the gospel and have enrolled themselves as His disciples. Could such a task possibly be completed in the lifetime of the original disciples? Of course not! Thus, Jesus is addressing Himself to every disciple in every era. When our Lord gave this charge to the disciples standing before Him in the first century, He, at the same time, gave it to every disciple who would follow in their steps. Therefore, we must be sure that we make Jesus' last words one of our first priorities.

Commentators Jamieson, Faussett, and Brown nicely summarize this matter when they say concerning our Lord's Great Commission words in Matthew 28:

> Now, was all this meant to be done by the Eleven men nearest to Him of the multitude then crowding around the risen Redeemer? Impossible. Was it to be done even in their lifetime? Surely not. In that little band Jesus virtually addressed Himself to all who, in every age, should take up from them the same work. Before the eyes of the church's risen Head were spread out, in those Eleven men, all His servants of every age; and one and all of them received His commission at that moment.[8]

Election and Evangelism: Friends or Foes?

Someone might object to this worldwide scope of evangelism on the grounds of the doctrine of election. How can it be

8 Jamieson, Faussett, and Brown, *A Commentary, Critical, Experimental, and Practical on the Old and New Testaments,* Matt. to Rev., Grand Rapids, MI: Eerdmans Publishing, 1982. 134.

possible for a person who holds to the biblical teaching of election also to believe that we are to share the gospel with all people? If we believe that only a certain number of people are going to be saved, how is it that we should preach to all? Have you ever heard these objections? Perhaps you have even thought them yourself.

Believing that God has an elect people whom He will save through the preaching of the gospel is not at all contrary to preaching the gospel to all men. *And why*? Because it is through the preaching of the gospel that the elect hear and are saved (Acts 13:42–14:1; 1 Cor. 1:21; 2 Tim. 2:8-10). We don't know who the elect are, but as we saw in the last chapter, our job is to preach to all people, not to convert anyone. This is what Spurgeon meant when he famously said, "If God would have painted a yellow stripe on the backs of the elect I would go around lifting shirts. But since He didn't, I must preach 'whosoever will' and when 'whosoever' believes I know that he is one of the elect."

This is why there is no inconsistency between reformed soteriology and biblical evangelism. In fact, it is the most consistent thing in the world when we understand that evangelism is the means God uses to bring His foreordained people to Himself. Election is the great incentive for evangelism, not a hindrance. This is what makes it exciting to be involved in the work, for if the Lord did not have a people who would be saved through the preaching of the gospel, that would kill our zeal. But since He does, this motivates and energizes us! Paul understood this plainly. After ministering in Corinth for many months with some success, he found himself once again being vehemently opposed by the Jews (Acts 18:6). In this challenging moment, the apostle had to decide: Should he stay in the city or leave? Should he labor there or pack his bags? Given the mounting trouble, what hope was there for further success? The answer came directly from the Lord Jesus Christ Himself, rooted in the doctrine of election. Despite the bleakness of Paul's situation, like a ray of light, his Savior offered encouragement through this profound biblical teaching. Jesus says to Paul:

> Do not be afraid, but speak, and do not keep silent; for I am with you, and no one will attack you to hurt you; for I have many people in this city (Acts 18: 9-10).

It's striking that Jesus referred to having "many people" in the city of Corinth *even before they were saved*. The point is, these individuals were already marked out, handpicked, and chosen by God to be His own "before the foundation of the world" (Eph. 1:4). How then did Paul respond to this revelation from his Savior? Did it persuade him to persevere in his gospel labors? The answer is clear: "And he continued there a year and six months, teaching the word of God among them" (Acts 18:11).

Further, this is why if you look into church history, you will also see that the greatest evangelists and missionaries were all reformed in their theology and held to the doctrine of election. The Puritans, George Whitefield, Charles Spurgeon, Jonathan Edwards, John Eliot, David Brainerd, William Carey, Adoniram Judson, and Martyn Lloyd-Jones are just a few.

Also, contrary to popular caricatures, even John Calvin was zealous about evangelism and did more for the promotion of the gospel than many of his critics, whether alive or dead: "Calvin made Geneva the base camp for an intensive evangelistic effort in France. Between 1555 and 1562 Calvin and his colleagues sent eighty-eight evangelists to France. God blessed their efforts because by 1559 the Huguenots (French

Calvinists) numbered over one hundred thousand. In 1555 Calvin commissioned a missionary to go to Brazil. All of this reflected Calvin's understanding of the Great Commission."[9] When commenting on Matthew 28:19, Calvin said, "The boundaries of Judea were prescribed to the prophets under the law, but now the wall is pulled down and the Lord orders the ministers of the gospel to go far out to scatter the teaching of salvation throughout all the regions of the earth."[10]

In John 4:35, our Lord Jesus says with reference to reaching out to the lost, "Behold I say to you, lift up your eyes and look at the fields for they are already white for harvest!" Reader, have you looked out recently? Have you considered the task at hand concerning the scope of evangelism either locally or overseas? Has it moved you to cry to God and say, "Oh, Lord, give me help to do all that you have called me to do." May this be the case for all of us.

For Reflection and Discussion

- Based on what we considered in this chapter, who will be the scope of your evangelistic efforts?
- Why is this to be the case concerning evangelism?
- Who do you have the most personal difficulty witnessing to and why? What will you do to overcome this?
- Is the Great Commission still in force today, and if so, why?

---

9 John Mark Terry, *Evangelism: A Concise History* (New York: Broadman & Holman, 1994), 79.

10 Timothy George, "The Challenges of Evangelism in the History of the Church," in *Evangelism in the Twenty-First Century*, ed. Thom Rainer (Wheaton, Ill.: Harold Shaw Publishers, 1989), 14.

3

The Motive for Biblical Evangelism

The salvation of men is a grand aim, but it must always be in subordination to the glory of the Lord, that His arm may be revealed, and that all flesh may see it together.

—Charles Spurgeon

Now that we understand that we are all called to share the gospel with everyone everywhere, what is our main motivation for doing so? What should compel us to witness to the lost, especially since this is not an easy task? In grasping the motive of biblical evangelism, we are addressing both a vertical and horizontal dimension: the glory of God (vertical) and the good of man (horizontal).[1]

Both dimensions are essential, but the primary focus must always be God's glory, out of which should flow a concern for man's good. Unfortunately, this is a place where

1 Ernest C. Reisinger also discusses this matter in his book *Today's Evangelism: Its Message and Methods* (Phillipsburg: P&R Publishing, 1982), 2-4.

many people go astray. They do this by putting the horizontal dimension first, which often leads to the use of gimmicks, pragmatism, and a compromised gospel message. In this horizontal or man-centered model, our evangelism becomes about what best caters to the lost. Such an approach truncates the gospel's message and discourages us from evangelizing if and when our efforts aren't producing "fruit," as we saw in chapter one.

The Glory of God

But what is God's glory? God's glory speaks of the intrinsic value, honor, and supreme worth that is associated with and manifested by His divine person and presence. It includes all that is connected to His names, titles, character, attributes, Word, and works, which flow from all that He is and all that He does. It refers to such "essential aspects of His being as excellency, dignity, worthiness, greatness, or beauty."[2] The Chronicler spoke about this in 2 Chronicles 5:14 when he said, "The glory of the Lord filled the house of God." The psalmist picks up this same theme in Psalm 19: "The heavens declare the glory of God; and the firmament shows his handiwork" (19:1). The great Dutch theologian, Herman Bavinck, summarized the subject well in his *Reformed Dogmatics*:

> The "glory of the Lord" is the splendor and brilliance that is inseparably associated with all of God's attributes and his self-revelation in nature and grace, the glorious form in which he everywhere appears to his creatures. This glory and majesty … appeared to Israel … It filled the tabernacle and

2 John D. Hannah, *How do we glorify God?* Basics of the Reformed Faith Series *How do we glorify God?* Phillipsburg, NJ: P&R Publishing, 2008, 11.

> the temple … and was communicated to all people … This glory is above all manifested in Christ, the only-begotten Son … and through him in the church … which is looking for "the blessed hope and the manifestation of the glory of our great God and Savior, Jesus Christ" (Titus 2:13).[3]

Given this understanding of the glory of God, it becomes clear why this vertical dimension is paramount in evangelism. As we have seen, Scripture teaches that salvation is solely of the Lord (Jonah 2:9). It also teaches that all of our actions are to be done for God's glory alone: "Therefore, whether you eat or drink, or whatever you do, *do all to the glory of God*" (1 Cor. 10:31). When evangelism is carried out for this primary reason, it perfectly aligns with this principle. Moreover, since evangelism is the main means through which God's redemptive plan for humanity comes to pass, when people come to faith in Christ, it results in them praising "the glory" of His grace shown towards them (Eph. 1:6). Therefore, having God's glory as the first motivation in our evangelism means that our primary drive is to honor and exalt Him through the gospel message we share rather than concentrating solely on the benefits for individuals. It ensures that our efforts remain centered on God and His eternal redemptive purposes in Christ rather than on ourselves or anything else.

But even if no one is saved, *God is still glorious*. Whether God saves a person or not, it doesn't detract from who He is. Further, there will be days when our love and passion for souls will wane or our fear of man will be high. In such

3 Herman Bavinck, *Reformed Dogmatics*, vol. 2, *God and Creation*, ed. John Bolt, trans. John Vriend (Grand Rapids: Baker Academic, 2004), 252.

times, we need more than just the horizontal or man-oriented dimension to drive us to reach the lost.

Consider this from the perspective of church history. How many examples do we have of evangelism being done for God's glory, even when few conversions occurred? Speaking of his early missionary work in India, William Carey said: "I am very fruitless and almost useless, but the Word and the attributes of God are my hope, and my confidence, and my joy, and I trust that his glorious designs will undoubtedly be answered."[4] If Carey's motives were mainly man-centered, he would have either left the mission field due to discouragement or he would have changed his methods and message in order to accommodate such difficult soil. This is what we see far too often in our own day. J. I. Packer highlights this point. He says that many Christians would quit evangelizing if not motivated by this vertical dimension of God's glory: "It is the only thing that gives us the resilience that we need if we are to evangelize boldly and persistently, and not be daunted by temporary setbacks."[5]

The greatest example of this vertical motive is seen in Jesus Himself. He saw few converts after three long years of ministry. When reading through the gospels, we even get the impression that at least half of Judea thought He was a madman (John 10:20). We know that our Lord's evangelism was also motivated by the horizontal dimension concerning man's good, but what sustained Him throughout His turbulent ministry was not this but that He "came down

---

4 William Carey to Mary Carey and Ann Hobson, December 22, 1796, in *The Journal and Selected Letters of William Carey*, ed. Terry G. Carter (Macon, Ga.: Smyth & Helwys, 2000), 249.

5 Packer, *Evangelism and the Sovereignty of God*, 10.

from heaven, not to do mine own will, but the will of Him that sent me" (John 6:38). Jesus told the disciples, "'My food is to do the will of Him who sent Me, and to finish His work'" (John 4:34). Before our Lord went to the cross, He said in His high priestly prayer to His Father in heaven, "I have glorified You on the earth. I have finished the work which you have given me to do" (John 17:4). Clearly, then, above all else, what motivated Jesus' earthly mission was the glory of God.

This idea of evangelizing for God's glory is inseparably connected to our love for God. We love Him because He first loved us (1 John 4:19). We love Him because, in love, He saved us and reconciled us to Himself. One reason that we share the gospel is as the hymn writer said, "It did so much for me, and that is just the reason I tell it now to thee."[6] Our "love for God" can be demonstrated in many ways, but one of the main ways is by our obedience to Him. For instance, Jesus says in John 14:15, "If you love Me, keep My commandments." The words "love Me" are inextricably joined to doing what He has commanded. You can't have one without the other. In 1 John 5:3, we are told, "For this is the love of God, that we keep His commandments."

Consequently, when we speak about bringing glory to God and loving Him, one of the ways we do this is by doing the work that God has called us to do. For example, this would include husbands loving their wives and wives respecting their husbands (Eph. 5:22-33). It includes laboring honestly at our jobs and forgiving our enemies (Col. 3:22-24; Matt. 6:14-15). But as we saw in the previous chapter, it also includes carrying out the great call of evangelism. When we evangelize the lost, we are being obedient to God, and such

6 "I Love to Tell the Story", Kate Hankey.

obedience glorifies Him. When we share Christ with others, we honor God's command and showcase His infinite love, mercy, and grace to a lost and dying world. Both of these things are accomplished when we do the work of evangelism. Consequently, Ernest Reisinger is correct when he asks,

> "How do we glorify God?" We glorify God by doing His will — and it is His will that we spread His name and His message of His salvation … He has given us the work of taking His message to all the world, thus our first motive must be love to God and concern for His glory. This is expressed in obedience to His revealed will. Therefore, if we are obedient to spreading God's message, He will be glorified regardless of the results.[7]

The Horizontal Dimension

The second motive of evangelism flows out of the vertical. This is called the "horizontal" dimension. So, what is this horizontal dimension of evangelism? As stated earlier, it is a concern for man's good. All biblical evangelism must have this component. We can claim to love God and His glory all we want, but if we don't have a genuine care for sinners, especially concerning their never-dying souls, then we are nothing more than noisy gongs and clanging cymbals. At this point, we are no better than the Pharisees, who, with all of their religiosity, didn't have love for the lost (Matt. 23:13). Biblical evangelism must be marked by genuine affection and tenderness for souls, which is driven by a profound love and concern for them. We must sincerely desire the salvation of our fellow mortals. We must be moved by a passion to see them delivered from the wrath to come, saying with Jeremiah of old:

---

7 Reisinger, *Today's Evangelism*, 3.

> I would comfort myself in sorrow; My heart is faint in me.
> Listen! The voice, The cry of the daughter of my people
> From a far country: "Is not the LORD in Zion?
> Is not her King in her?" "Why have they provoked Me to anger With their carved images—With foreign idols?" "The harvest is past, The summer is ended,
> And we are not saved!" For the hurt of the daughter of my people I am hurt.
> I am mourning; Astonishment has taken hold of me. Is there no balm in Gilead, Is there no physician there? Why then is there no recovery for the health of the daughter of my people? Oh, that my head were waters, And my eyes a fountain of tears, That I might weep day and night For the slain of the daughter of my people! (Jer. 8:18–9:1).

Further, we must also be like Jude, who said, "Others save with fear, pulling them out of the fire hating even the garment defiled by the flesh" (Jude 23). We must long to see our friends, family, coworkers, and even enemies reconciled to God through the good news of Jesus Christ. Such a motive for evangelism is critical. In fact, without this love for souls, we don't glorify God, who "desires" that all kinds of people will be "saved and to come to the knowledge of the truth" (1 Tim. 2:4).

As with the vertical motive, the most outstanding example of this horizontal concern for souls is Jesus Christ Himself. When Jesus was criticized for hanging out with "sinners," He remarks that "those who are well have no need of a physician, but those who are sick. I did not come to call the righteous, but sinners, to repentance" (Mark 2:17). Elsewhere He said that He came into the world "to seek and to save that which was lost" (Luke 19:10). When He thought about the impenitence of his own countrymen He wept, "O Jerusalem, Jerusalem, the one who kills the prophets and stones those who are sent to her! How often I would have gathered your children together, as a hen gathers her chicks under her wings, but you were not willing!" (Matt. 23:37). Christ is the Great Physician, and this is particularly evidenced in His concern for diseased, sin-sick souls. His purpose for coming to earth was to lay down His life as a ransom for many (Mark 10:45). In His coming to earth, He glorifies God, but that is because it is inextricably tied up with His great mission to save men and women from their sins (Matt. 1:21).

Such a love and compassion for souls can also be found in the Apostle Paul. This is especially seen in the following passage from Romans: "I tell the truth in Christ, I am not lying, my conscience also bearing me witness in the Holy Spirit, that I have great sorrow and continual grief in my heart. For I could wish that I myself were accursed from Christ for my brethren, my countrymen according to the flesh" (Rom. 9:1-3). At first glance, Paul's love for his countrymen seems entirely normal. Who doesn't have natural affection for his own people? But upon closer inspection, such a love for his countrymen is anything but natural, considering the treatment he has received from their hands. These are the people who had him stoned, beaten with rods, whipped, and, on several occasions, tried to condemn him through the legal system of the time (2 Cor. 11:22-33). By the end of his life, they would succeed in having him arrested upon false charges (see Acts 24–26). How many nights in prison did Paul spend because of these "countrymen"? How many close calls with death? How many lost comforts? If anyone had a reason to wish people were not saved, it would have been Paul. But far from being jaded or resentful towards them, he would instead be cut off from God rather than to see his countrymen cut off!

Here, he says that he was willing to do whatever it took if it meant that his unsaved fellow Jews would escape the judgment of God. He was willing to "lose anything and everything if they but be saved," as Spurgeon said. Paul says with a heart of compassion that although he knew that he could never actually atone for the sins of others or be cut off for them, nonetheless, out of his love for them, he would gladly change places if he could with these people who have made his life a storm of heartache and controversy everywhere he went. His heart throbs with love for them. He can't fathom the thought of them not being saved and going to hell forever. This is what earnestly compels the apostle to labor and pray for them, "Brethren, my heart's desire and prayer to God for Israel is that they may be saved" (Rom. 10:1). This motivates him to continue sharing Christ with them, regardless of the treatment he receives at their hands. Yes, God is absolutely sovereign in salvation and His glory is preeminent above all else. But there are souls around the apostle who are dying in their sin, and he longs to see them reconciled to God. Therefore, the two aspects are not contradictory. They work together.

How to Love Our Fellow Man

What is the most loving thing we can do for our neighbor? Material gifts are nice, as well as meals and showing hospitality. But if the person dies in their sins, without Christ, all the material comforts in the world would mean nothing. The most loving thing we can do for our neighbors is speak to them about the Savior. Sharing the gospel with them is the kindest act we can do because it addresses their deepest need—the need for deliverance from the penalty of sin and God's wrath and a real relationship with Him through Jesus Christ the Lord.

But what happens if our neighbor rejects our efforts to bring him the gospel? What if we are looked down upon or ridiculed? It helps to remember that Paul experienced this, too. So did Jesus. This is nothing new. Christ told us, "If the world hates you, you know that it hated Me before it hated you" (John 15:18).

But even better, what if the person you evangelize gets converted? What if your efforts are used by God to bring about his or her salvation? As we saw in chapter one, faith comes by hearing, and so the only way for souls to be saved is by someone going to them with the gospel. They may throw something at you or curse you out. However, more likely, they will simply look at you oddly and go on their way. But isn't this better than them not knowing about the grace of God in Christ through the gospel? If they are to enter into hell, let it be with a thousand gospel arrows stuck in their backs. Or, as Spurgeon said: "If sinners will be damned, at least let them leap to Hell over our dead bodies. And if they perish, let them perish with our arms about their knees, imploring them to stay. If Hell must be filled, let it be filled in the teeth of our exertions, and let not one go unwarned and unprayed for."[8]

Isn't this why Paul kept preaching even when persecuted (Acts 14:19-21)? Isn't this what motivated Jesus, even when He knew His own people would by and large reject Him (John 1:11)? These men were driven by a love for souls.

---

8 2200 *Quotations from the writings of Charles H. Spurgeon*, Tom Carter, Compiler, Grand Rapids, MI: Baker Books, 1988, 67.

I am convinced that a helpful way to warm cold hearts to evangelize is to soberly assess the everlasting agonies of hell. Doing this will prod us to speak to people about Jesus. Think, dear reader, of the unending flames of hell. Think of the wrath of Almighty God pressing down upon the lost without end, where "the smoke of their torment ascends forever and ever, and they have no rest day or night" (Rev. 14:11). Think of the great worth of the human soul. Jesus said that its value is worth more than the whole world, for "what profit is it to a man if he gains the whole world, and loses his own soul?" (Matt. 16:26).

Even certain atheists have understood the importance of evangelism in light of our belief in hell. Consider this quote from well-known magician and atheist Penn Jillette:

> I've always said that I don't respect people who don't proselytize. I don't respect that at all. If you believe that there's a heaven and a hell, and people could be going to hell or not getting eternal life, and you think that it's not really worth telling them this because it would make it socially awkward—and atheists who think people shouldn't proselytize and who say just leave me alone and keep your religion to yourself—how much do you have to hate somebody to *not* proselytize? How much do you have to hate somebody to believe everlasting life is possible and not tell them that? I mean, if I believed, beyond the shadow of a doubt, that a truck was coming at you, and you didn't believe that truck was bearing down on you, there is a certain point where I tackle you. And this is *more* important than that.[9]

Reader, do you believe in the eternal horrors of hell? Do you believe the gospel alone is the message that can save a

9 *A Gift of a Bible*. YouTube, July 8, 2010.

person from it? Do you believe God uses means, especially people like you, to convey that message to lost souls? Do you love your neighbor? Then be bold to share the gospel with others! Don't let your love for others be submerged beneath the weight of self-love or self-preservation. No, rather let gospel compassion swallow your fears! How often do we neglect to share the gospel with others because we love our comfort, security, and status more than we love lost sinners? A little discomfort for us in this life doesn't compare to the great discomfort of the one who goes to hell. This is why Paul could say, "Knowing, therefore, the terror of the Lord, we persuade men" (2 Cor. 5:11).

Biblical Evangelism Is Both Vertical and Horizontal

God, in His providence, has placed us in our families, communities, jobs, and era of history. All around us are people on their way to the "judgment seat of Christ, that each one may receive the things done in the body according to what he has done, whether good or bad" (2 Cor. 5:10). If you love God's glory and God Himself for saving you, you will also love telling lost souls about the Savior. If you love lost souls, you will evangelize in accordance with how God has prescribed it. Thus, biblical evangelism is the fusion of the vertical and horizontal dimensions. When these two dimensions come together, they create a powerful motivation that can overcome any obstacle. The desire to glorify God and the love for others constrains us to reach out, even when it's difficult. Therefore, may God help us all to be busy with this most sacred work of evangelism for the glory of our great King and for the sake of the lost.

For Reflection and Discussion

- What are the twofold motivating aspects of our evangelistic efforts?
- What is the glory of God?
- Why is evangelism the greatest kindness we can do toward the lost?
- Who, in the Bible or church history, motivates you to speak to others about their great need for salvation?

4

The Agents of Biblical Evangelism

Every single believer is a God-ordained agent of evangelism.

—R. B. Kuiper

In chapter one, we learned that God uses people to share the gospel with others, and through this process, souls are saved. In other words, God uses means! Let us now dig deeper into this remarkable fact, exploring it both theologically and practically.

God Prescribes, Not Man

When it comes to how we are to worship the one true and living God, we are to go to His Word for His instruction and direction to see what He says about it. How does God want to be worshiped? What does biblical worship look like according to the Almighty? This approach to worship has historically been called the "regulative principle" of worship. Regulative worship means that Scripture alone regulates what we do or don't do in the corporate worship of God, and it avoids appealing to fads, trends, or human ingenuity.[1] This practice is contrasted with what is commonly called the "normative principle" of worship. Normative worship means that anything that God has not expressly forbidden is permissible in worship, and so it tends to lean more heavily on innovative and creative approaches to corporate worship.

Sadly, as our current Christian culture shows, this second view of worship has opened up a Pandora's Box when it comes to what is done in God's house on any given Sunday. What is more, considering how vital the proper worship of God is, we would be utterly foolish to assume that He would leave what is proper or improper in His sight up to our fallen understanding, ingenuity, whims, and personal preferences. Thus, the "regulative principle" is the appropriate approach to the worship of God.[2]

The same holds true for evangelism. Although there are different ways to evangelize (as we will see in this chapter), this does not mean that God hasn't given us clear principles from His Word about what evangelism is and how it should be done. For instance, we noticed that evangelism is done primarily through people. In God's good will, He has ordained the use of humans to further His glorious good news to others (2 Cor. 4:7). God has tasked His people to take the message of Christ to the lost around them. God has chosen us to be the channels through which His saving truth would come to them. We are God's method!

---

1 Two recent helpful works on this subject are Sam Waldron's *How Then Should We Worship?* and D. Scott Meadow's *A Call to Pure Worship*.

2 The historic Confessions of the Christian faith, such as The 1689 London Baptist Confession of Faith (2LBCF) and The Westminster Confession of Faith (WCF), bear this out as well, see 2LBCF 22; WCF 21.

If such a fact seems too remarkable to be true, that's the whole point. The reason God has designed things this way is not because of how great we are as human beings. It's not because of our exceptional wisdom or gifting compared to other creatures he might have used. In fact, the reverse is the case. God uses us as His instruments because we are utterly incapable of handling such a gospel, except by His mercy and grace alone. That God uses us to be His tools in the task of evangelism should astonish and humble us. In His wisdom, He has decreed it proper to use pitiful, redeemed, sinful creatures like us to speak the gospel to lost people on His behalf. In this way, God shows that any good fruit must be all of Him, *not us*. As we see rebels repent and come to the Savior, God demonstrates that He alone is the source of their salvation (Rev. 7:10). We, as mere creatures, could never have brought it about. Thus, as we saw in the last chapter, this approach ensures that God alone receives all the glory and praise (1 Cor. 1:26-31).

To consider this more deeply, let's revisit Peter's encounter with Cornelius, the centurion. In Acts 10, an angel of God comes to Cornelius and tells him to call on Peter so that he can come to Cornelius's house and tell them "words by which you and your household will be saved" (Acts 11:14). But why didn't the angel simply communicate the gospel directly to Cornelius? Why go through the process of sending Cornelius's men to Joppa to get Peter, and then have Peter travel to Cornelius's house, and share what could've been done by the angel on the spot? Why did God have the angel tell Cornelius to send for Peter? God could've just written across the sky, "believe on the Lord Jesus Christ and you will be saved," but He didn't. He could've instantly popped the gospel into their minds, but He chose not to. Why? Because God has chosen men and women as His means to accomplish the task of evangelism. Even though God employs angels in various ways, He has chosen to use us as His agents of good when it comes to lost souls. He could've easily brought about His work of salvation without instruments, but He has decreed that "faith comes by hearing" (Rom. 10:17).

There are a number of other passages which proclaim the same truth. Peter tells us that the church is "a chosen generation, a royal priesthood, a holy nation, His own special people," and that in light of this, *we are to* "proclaim the praises of Him who called [us] out of darkness into His marvelous light" (1 Pet. 2:9). In Matthew, we see Jesus sending the disciples "into the highways," instructing them by way of a parable, and saying, "and as many as you find, invite to the wedding" (Matt. 22:9). In Luke, Jesus brings in a large haul of fish for Peter, but He then turns it into another parable for Peter's new assignment: "From now on you will catch men" (Luke 5:10). Additionally in Acts, we see that an angel commissions Philip to go toward Gaza where he will encounter the Ethiopian eunuch. Upon approaching, the Spirit *tells him to* "overtake this chariot" (Acts 8:29). Philip proceeds to share Christ with the eunuch from Isaiah chapter 53, and the eunuch is saved and then is baptized (Acts 8:34-38). This is just a sampling of what the Scriptures tell us regarding the instrumentality of human beings when it comes to evangelism. With this biblical foundation firmly established, let's look at one passage in particular that illuminates the role that humans have in God's plan for evangelism: 1 Corinthians 3.

1 Corinthians 3 and Evangelism

In this passage, Paul is dealing with the issue of divisions in the church (1 Cor. 3:1-4). A sectarian spirit had emerged around different leaders, including Paul and Apollos. Both of these men, even today, are considered pillars of the church. They have had huge reputations for the last two thousand years, and the same was true in the early church. And yet, this factious spirit was dividing the believers around a shameful cult of personalities.

There were many approaches Paul could have taken to correct this attitude. The one he chose, however, was to ask the church (which was founded through his ministry during his second missionary journey cf. Acts 18), "Who then is Paul, and who is Apollos, but ministers through whom you believed, as the Lord gave to each one?" (1 Cor. 3:5). Here, Paul tells us two things about himself and Apollos. First, neither one of them is worth fighting over. They are merely men, not the heads of rival schools. Regardless of their ministries' success, they were dust and bones, nothing else. Second, he says that it was through them that the Corinthian church believed the gospel. In other words, it was through the gospel message proclaimed by Paul and Apollos that the church in Corinth heard the Word of God, and by God's grace and power they believed it to the saving of their souls.

Again, consider what Paul is doing here. He didn't say that he and Apollos were the objects of the Corinthians' faith. Instead, he says they were simply the means God used to bring them the message. They were ministers, or even better translated, "servants through whom you believed." This is precisely why it would be heinous to build a following around them. The message was not about them but about Christ, "the Lord," who gave "each one" of them the fruit of their ministries and the ability to minister accordingly (1 Cor. 3:5b).

Also, Paul does not say he and Apollos were servants "from whom" they believed, as though they were the source of their faith. Not at all! Rather, he says that they were the God-ordained channels through which they came to faith in Christ, and by which God did His saving work among the Corinthians. Paul emphasizes this in the following verse: "I planted, Apollos watered, but God gave the increase" (1 Cor. 3:6). Therefore, Christ is the one they were to follow, not Paul or Apollos, and yet God used Paul and Apollos as instruments for bringing them to faith. "So then neither he who plants is anything, nor he who waters, but God who gives the increase" (1 Cor. 3:7). This point is again repeated in Paul's second letter to the Corinthians: "Now all things are of God, who has reconciled us to Himself through Jesus Christ, and has given us the ministry of reconciliation, that is, that God was in Christ reconciling the world to Himself, not imputing their trespasses to them, and has committed to us the word of reconciliation. Now then we are ambassadors for Christ, as though God were pleading through us: we implore you on Christ's behalf, be reconciled to God" (2 Cor. 5:18-20).

Thus, *evangelism is to be done by people, to people, and for people.* Although the Lord is the only one who can sovereignly transform a person's heart, when we share God's saving truth, we play a vital part. This is why it is crucial that we are not apathetic when it comes to the duty of evangelism. We are the unique agents God uses to plead with men to be reconciled to Him.

How then are you, dear reader, contributing your time and energy to the task and responsibility of evangelism? How are you being used by God for souls? What are some ways that you can go about doing evangelism? Are you speaking to people about Christ? Are you getting to know people for the sake of seeing a door opened for evangelism? Are you reaching out to the people in your neighborhoods and your places of work? Are you asking God to open doors in your life to share the gospel?

Away with Hyper-Calvinism and Forward with the Gospel!
Converts are made through evangelism. Although salvation is entirely of the Lord, it is done through human beings telling other human beings about Christ. This is why hyper-Calvinism, the belief that God saves sinners without means or human involvement, is to be rejected wherever it rears its ugly head. Any notion of God not calling on us to be involved in the work of the Great Commission, which includes but is not limited to evangelism, must be dismissed as unbiblical. Also, the idea that God only uses ministers, not laymen or "ordinary" Christians, is inconsistent with biblical revelation. For instance, Acts 8:4 tells us that "those who were scattered went everywhere preaching the word." We know these were not the apostles because we are told they stayed behind in Jerusalem (Acts 8:1). Rather, these were laymen from the church sharing the gospel with others.

As God's redeemed people, we all have our work cut out for us regarding evangelism. All Christians are to be involved in the work, even if all are not called to be involved in it in the same way. Not all are called to preach open-air on campuses or street corners. Not all are called to engage in door-to-door evangelism. Mothers can evangelize their children at home and employees their coworkers. When we're at a restaurant, we can drop off a gospel tract with our generous tip, or we can start an evangelistic Bible study in our homes. We all have neighbors whom we are to love as ourselves (Matt. 22:39), and what is more loving than to tell a lost soul about the forgiveness of sins, reconciliation with God, and the glories of Christ as found in the gospel? The point is we are all called to do something for the Lord concerning evangelism.

Such a perspective as this is the proper response to the gospel in our lives. Evangelizing doesn't earn us merit in the eyes of God. We aren't saved by how much we evangelize. Rather, because Christ has given His all for us, we ought to be willing to give our all for Him, which includes telling others about Him and what He has done for us.

"Whom Shall I Send, and Who Will Go for Us?"

The idea of loving our neighbor as ourselves is crucial because when we see the state of our culture today, we should also see that the culture is just a collective of human beings, and human beings are lost. Paul describes them as "strangers from the covenants of promise, having no hope and without God in the world" (Eph. 2:12). Do you remember what it was like to have no hope and no God while in the world? That is the description of most people in our cities, neighborhoods, and places of work. They are under God's wrath. They are living without understanding their true purpose. Their sin does not make them victims, but it does make them candidates to hear about Jesus. Their only hope in life and death is the gospel. The only remedy for their lost estate is Jesus Christ saving them through the power of the Holy Spirit as the gospel's message goes forth from our lips to their hearts.

But who is going to share this message with them? Who is going to reach the lost people in your life? Will it be the Mormons, Jehovah's Witnesses, or the Marxists in the universities? The truth is that people are reaching such folks every day with false hopes and false gospels, which are deceiving their souls. But we have the truth as it is found in Christ! Who is going to tell them about Him? The answer, of course, is us! Whether they get converted isn't up to us, but the sharing part is. Isn't it amazing that God has entrusted us with this all-important task of evangelizing the lost? Consequently, as Paul says, let us be people who "endure all things for the sake of the elect, that they also may obtain the salvation that is in Christ Jesus with eternal glory" (2 Tim. 2:10).

But What Is the Best Approach to Evangelism?

Now that it has been established from Scripture that God uses humans to share the gospel, we are ready to look at some practical ways to do it briefly. Concerning this matter, it is essential to recognize that evangelism can take many forms, be done in many contexts, and still be biblical. Evangelism is not a one-size-fits-all endeavor. Whether it's open-air preaching, one-on-one conversations, distributing tracts, hosting an evangelistic Bible study, or going door-to-door, God can use each of these approaches and others to advance the gospel. No method should be treated as the best, nor should any method be looked down on, provided one crucial condition is met: the biblical gospel remains central in every encounter and is clearly communicated. This is the key to the whole point and must always be the priority in any evangelistic effort.

God uses people in different ways to spread His truth and has uniquely gifted individuals to reach others. Yet again, the most important thing is that His truth is being spread. Therefore, assuming that people are staying within the scope of Scripture in their evangelistic message, we should rejoice in seeing the gospel go forth, even if it's in ways different from our own.

For Reflection and Discussion

- According to the Bible, what is the main means when it comes to evangelizing the lost?
- What are some key passages in the Bible that prove this point?
- What is hyper-Calvinism, and why should it be rejected?
- Concerning evangelism, what is the central thing that must always be true regardless of the various approaches in which it may be done?

5

The Message of Biblical Evangelism

For I am not ashamed of the gospel of Christ, for it is the power of God to salvation for everyone who believes, for the Jew first and also for the Greek.

—The Apostle Paul (Rom. 1:16)

We have reached the thrilling heart of this book. Up to now, we have explored why the gospel is needed, who it should reach, what should drive us to share it, and through whom it should be communicated. Now, let's tackle the most vital question: What exactly is the "gospel"? According to the Bible, what are the main aspects of this word, which, as mentioned in chapter one, means "good news?"[1]

1 It should be noted that the term *gospel* in its biblical-historical use is found in the Septuagint, and it refers to the Old Testament footmen who announced the "good news" of freedom from Babylonian captivity in the sixth century B.C. (cf. Isa. 52:7-10; Rom. 10:15). As these Jewish exiles traveled over the mountains back to Jerusalem, these heralds zealously went before the people, announcing this joyful and exciting news. Further, scholars tell us that the term "gospel" was

Unlike previous generations, our present age is relatively uneducated concerning this crucial question. In a time like ours, the irony is stark—the most important message in all the universe is almost entirely unknown to many outside the church and, sadly, even to some within it.

In asking your unsaved neighbors what the gospel is, you might hear, "It's the words of Jesus" or "It's the various books of the Bible." Some might think it means helping the poor or being kind to those who hurt you. Others might just shrug and admit they don't know.

Such confusion underscores the urgency of addressing this matter correctly, since the gospel is God's declaration from heaven of how individuals can be made right with Him through Jesus Christ the Lord. This chapter is dedicated to furthering the knowledge and clarity we need when communicating the gospel to the lost. Remember, the gospel is "the power of God to salvation for everyone who believes (Rom. 1:16). However, if we miscommunicate it, everything else about our evangelism will not matter. So, what exactly do we tell others when we share the gospel with them?

---

not invented by Paul but was already used in his day by the Romans regarding Roman imperial propaganda. In the first century, there was what was called the "good news" or "the gospel" of the Caesars. Such "good news" referred to an announcement of "glad tidings" regarding a birthday or a rise to power of the emperor that was to be known to all for hope for future days.

Having said these two things about the gospel, of course, the gospel that we share with others is much grander and more glorious than the aforementioned examples. For one thing, the gospel we preach is God's Emancipation Proclamation; it is a decree of freedom, not merely from physical enemies and oppression as was the case with the Hebrew exiles, but from spiritual enemies and spiritual oppression. And for another thing, the good news we proclaim is not about a mere man (such as Caesar), but rather about the all-powerful God-man, Jesus Christ, who alone is to be worshiped [a modified excerpt from Ventura, *Expository Outlines*, 24].

What are its key elements in its fuller theological sense? Broadly speaking, we can say that the major components of the gospel boil down to four core components: *God, the Righteous; Man, the rebel; Jesus, the Redeemer; and our Right Response to the message.*

The Gospel Is About God, *the Righteous*

When it comes to evangelism, the starting point of our message is essential. It can be easy for us to miss the mark here. For instance, should we start with sin? Or what about starting with man himself? While specific contexts may necessitate these beginnings, subjects such as sin and man can only be properly understood in their relationship to God. For instance, according to Scripture, sin is lawlessness (1 John 3:4). It is according to the Westminster Shorter Catechism, "any want [lack] of conformity unto or transgression of, the law of God" (Q. 14). God and His moral law, the Ten Commandments, are the standards of holiness for all people in all places, and at all times. They are the measurements of His righteousness. Consequently, sin cannot be rightly understood until one knows about the God of the Bible in whom there "is no darkness at all" (1 John 1:5), and His holy inflexible law, which brings "the knowledge of sin" (Rom. 3:20). God's law also promises eternal punishment in hell. This is because there is an eternal penalty connected to breaking it (Rom. 6:23a). Therefore, Luther was right when he said that the function of the law is "not to justify but to terrify."

The same is true of man. Man cannot understand himself until he first understands his relationship to God, his Creator. Man is a created being (Gen. 2:7). He is not the master of his own destiny nor the definer of right and wrong.

As a creature of God, man is obliged to love God with all his heart, soul, mind, and strength (Mark 12:30). Moreover, he is required to keep God's law perfectly, perpetually, and personally if he would ever be accepted by Him (Gal. 3:10; James 1:10). *However, man has failed to do this.* This is why the gospel message must initially focus on God and His law against whom man has sinned so that he can first see the bad news of his lost condition.

Consider Romans 1:18. After mentioning the gospel in the previous words of Romans 1:16-17, Paul now states, "For the wrath of God is revealed from heaven against all ungodliness and unrighteousness of men who suppress the truth in unrighteousness." Notice here that along with beginning with God, Paul doesn't start his gospel proclamation by saying, "God loves us and has a wonderful plan for our lives." Instead, he begins by declaring that because God is holy and man is *un*holy, His wrath is not merely toward him, but more literally, from the Greek text, it is *upon him*. In Romans 1:18, Paul explains why it is that every single person in the world needs the gospel, which is "the power of God unto salvation for everyone who believes for the Jew first and also the Greek" (Rom. 1:16). He also shows why it is that all people need "the righteousness of God" (Rom. 1:17), credited to their account to cover their unrighteousness, which righteousness is revealed in the gospel, received by faith alone, and is the perfect righteousness of Christ (Jer. 23:6; Rom. 5:15-19; 1 Cor. 1:30; 2 Cor. 5:21; Phil. 3:9).

In addition to God's wrath against the sinner, the Bible also reveals that the God of the Bible is holy, just, and our ultimate Judge. The Psalms declare, "The Lord our God is holy" (Ps. 99:9), and sinless angels cry out before God in glory night and day, saying, "Holy, holy, holy, is the LORD of hosts; the whole earth is full of His glory" (Isa. 6:3). Further, Psalm 89:14 states that "righteousness and justice" are the foundation of God's throne. And the Psalmist also says in Psalm 96:13 that God will "judge the world with righteousness, and the peoples with His truth."

These aspects of God are unpopular with modern listeners. However, they are crucial when sharing the gospel. If people don't recognize God for who He is in truth, then they will never understand the dire condition they are in or the profound love He showed in sending His Son, Jesus, to die for sinners like them. Too often, people try to present God as down-to-earth, relatable, and buddy-like so that individuals will be "attracted" to Him. However, the Bible never presents God in this manner. Rather, according to the Bible, God is utterly unique, unlike anything or anyone else in the universe. He is not like man; He is the Creator, while everything else is created by Him (Ps. 50:21). We must tell the lost about the biblical God. We must begin where Paul began his gospel presentation with the fact that outside of Christ, God is angry with us "every day" (Ps. 7:11) because of our sin against His holy Person and law. We must emphasize the fact that one day, everyone will appear before "the judgment seat of Christ, that each one may receive the things done in the body, according to what he has done, whether good or bad" (2 Cor. 5:10). Only then will the unsaved realize their desperate, deplorable, and hopeless situation before the holy God of the Bible, "with whom we have to do" (Heb. 4:13), and that only He Himself can deliver them from it. Only then will sinners greatly value and fully appreciate God's amazing grace and His glorious remedy for their enormous malady.

The Gospel Is About Man, *the Rebel*

This leads us to our next crucial aspect when sharing the gospel; it's not only a message about God, it's also a message about man. But what are we to say when it comes to man? Are we to tell unsaved individuals (both men and women) that they are basically good, and already on their way to heaven, and that they just need a little spiritual nudge in the right direction to be right with God? Or should we tell them they just need to try a little harder, be a little nicer, attend church more regularly, and then assure them that all will be well with them at last?

It might surprise some, but the Bible never encourages these things, nor does it ever aim to build up their self-esteem. Instead, it provides a stark and accurate assessment of their lost spiritual state. The Bible is a book of realism. It is the only book in all the world that presents us in truth. It alone gives us God's anthropology, showing unsaved humanity in all its native ugliness and total depravity. It shows that regardless of people's backgrounds, education, wealth, age, upbringing, skin color, gender, vocation, charisma, or anything else, they are inherently wicked by nature and practice. They are lost and dead in trespasses and sins (Eph. 2:1), self-absorbed, going astray as soon as they are born, and speaking lies (Ps. 58:3). They are darkened in their understanding, being alienated from the life of God because of the ignorance that is in them because of the blindness of their hearts (Eph. 4:18). They are separated from God because of their sins against Him (Isa. 59:2). Although they know that God exists because their consciences and creation testify to it (Rom. 1:19), they are nonetheless living in rebellion to Him, not serving or living for Him. Instead they are seeking out many schemes (Eccles. 7:29), as they live at enmity against God (Rom. 8:7), turning everyone to his own way (Isa. 53:6). Consequently, they are all under His just wrath (John 3:36; Rom. 1:8).

This is the world we live in. These are the people we mingle with daily. This is humanity's condition apart from God's salvation.

This is the fact about rebellious mankind. It isn't pleasant, *but it's true nonetheless*. This is the bad news. Not only is God a righteous judge, but we are wicked lawbreakers who rightly deserve hell. To faithfully present the biblical gospel, we must make this part clear and upfront. People must understand the dreadful reality of their condition and the dire position they are in because of it. We must lovingly communicate to men and women the severity of the situation. When sharing the gospel, we must get to this point with our hearers.

The Gospel Is About Jesus, *the Redeemer*

Thankfully, the biblical gospel doesn't stop with us telling unbelievers that God must punish them in hell forever for their sins. Instead, having told them the bad news *first*, we now get to tell them the "good news," which makes it good news indeed! This good news is centered on Jesus—God's Son (Rom. 1:1-4) and in His substitutionary, sin-bearing work for the guilty (Isa. 53:6; 1 Cor. 15:1-4; 2 Cor. 5:21).

This is the heart of the gospel—*its core*. But here, too, we must understand what we need to communicate to the lost. When it comes to the good news of Jesus, two essential aspects must be established with the unbeliever: His Person and His work.

The person of Jesus Christ means much more than Him just being a religious leader with many profound things to say. And it's more than just acknowledging that He did many wonderful things on the earth. Rather, borrowing language from one historic Confession of Faith, we see that Jesus Christ is:

> The Son of God, the second person in the Holy Trinity, being very and eternal God, the brightness of the Father's glory, of one substance and equal with him who made the world, who upholds and governs all things he has made, did, when the fullness of time was come, take upon himself man's nature with all the essential properties and common infirmities thereof, yet without sin; being conceived by the Holy Spirit in the womb of the Virgin Mary, the Holy Spirit coming down upon her: and the power of the Most High overshadowing her; and so was made of a woman of the tribe of Judah, of the seed of Abraham and David according to the Scriptures; so that two whole, perfect, and distinct natures were inseparably joined together in one person, without conversion, composition, or confusion; which person is very God and very man, yet one Christ, the only mediator between God and man (2LBCF 8.2).

What a superb statement! In summary, it teaches us that Jesus Christ is very God, of very God, the Second Person of the Trinity. It teaches us that He is the Supreme Being who became a man.

We see these matters declared in multiple places in Scripture. At Jesus' birth, we are told, "He will be great and will be called the Son of the Highest" (Luke 1:32). The apostle John tells us concerning Jesus: "In the beginning was the Word, and the Word was with God, and the Word was God … And the Word became flesh and dwelt among us (John 1:1, 14). Paul describes Jesus in Romans 9:5, by saying that "Christ came, who is over all, the eternally blessed God." Additionally, he says to Timothy, "And without controversy great is the mystery of godliness: 'God was manifested in the flesh'" (1 Tim. 3:16).

However, understanding these grand truths about Jesus isn't enough when it comes to the biblical gospel. It is utterly astonishing that God the Son would willingly incarnate Himself (take on flesh), but why would He do so? What was the glorious purpose behind it? This brings us next to *the work of Jesus Christ.*

After telling us in Romans 3:19, 20, that God's law shows that all people outside of Christ are guilty before Him and that "by the deeds of the law no flesh will be justified in His sight," Paul then follows the pattern of bad news first then good news and summarizes the gospel message in Romans 3:23-25a, when he says:

> **for all** (i.e., each and every person Jew or Gentile) **have sinned** (that is, broken God's commandments in thought, word, and in deed), **and fall short of the glory** (not just a Law of God, but the moral glory and excellence) **of God, being justified** (or declared and reckon not guilty, i.e., forgiven) **freely** (without any cost or charge to us, without any works or merit or any performance on our part but simply as a gift) **by His grace** (or God's unmerited favor and kindness to those who do not deserve such things) **through the redemption** (that is, the payment price which was made to satisfy His divine justice for our sins against Him) **that is in** (the preposition "in" identifying the unique agent of our redemption), "**that is** in," (or connected to, and paid for exclusively by) **Christ** (the messiah) **Jesus, whom God** (that is to say, God the Father) **set forth *as* a propitiation** (a wrath-absorber who stopped His divine anger against us by His wrath-absorbing sacrifice in our place, which wrath-absorbing sacrifice Jesus was) **by His blood**, (that is, the blood of Christ, which speaks about His death which was the exclusive basis of the propitiation) **through faith** (not our good deeds, not baptism, not our law

> keeping) but "through faith" which puts forth the instrumental means by which God applies Jesus' work to our account.[2]

Our salvation (i.e., our deliverance from God's judgment) comes through the payment of death, but it wasn't just anyone's death—it was the death of the God-man, Jesus Christ. Only the God-man could fulfill the momentous task of bearing an eternal hell for us. Because God's justice demands that we must be punished for our sins, Jesus took that penalty in our stead. This is what is meant by "propitiation by His blood." The point is, Jesus has appeased God's wrath towards sinners by taking their sins upon His sinless self and enduring the full weight of divine wrath and punishment for them at the cross. Through Jesus, our sin and consequence before the Almighty is removed (Matt. 26:28). Through Jesus, the offended God is now reconciled to us (Rom. 5:11). *But how can we know this for sure?*

Jesus' resurrection from the dead validates the completion and acceptance of His atoning work for us on the cross, by His Father in heaven. Yes, Jesus died! But death and the grave could not hold Him! On the third day, He rose again marking God's stamp of approval of Christ's sacrifice (Rom. 4:25). Again, the historic Confession of Faith highlights this truth, stating that Jesus:

> underwent the punishment due to us, which we should have borne and suffered, being made sin and a curse for us; enduring most grievous sorrows in his soul, and most painful sufferings in his body; was crucified, and died, and remained in the state of the dead, yet saw no corruption: on the third day he arose from the dead with the same body in which he suffered, with which he also ascended into heaven … (2LBC 8.4).

---

2 Ventura, *Expository Outlines*, 99-101.

This is *what* makes the gospel "good news." This is *why* the gospel is great news! The gospel addresses the most serious problem we face: God is holy, we are not. His holiness and justice demands He punish our sins. However, in love, grace, and mercy, He provided a substitute—Jesus, who paid our sin penalty in full 2,000 years ago at Calvary. This is why Jesus declared from the cross, "It is finished!" (John 19:30). This is why the biblical gospel is not a message of what we must do to be made right with God. Rather it is a proclamation of what Jesus has already done to accomplish this for us. In this sense, then, we could say that the gospel is not a *what*, but a *who*. It is a message that ultimately revolves around God's Son; thus, Calvin was right when he said, "The whole gospel is contained in Christ."[3] Praise be to God!

The Gospel Is About *Our Right Response to the Message*

In considering the gospel, we must understand how the lost receive the benefits of Jesus' person and work. Is this automatic for them? Is it merely hearing the message that does it? Or is it by simply "accepting Jesus," as many tell us in our day? According to the Bible, what are the true terms with which sinners must comply? This leads us to the crucial fourth and final step: the response.

The gospel has a summons connected to it. It is not merely informational but rather it's a royal call from God, requiring sinners to take specific actions—namely, to repent of their sins and believe the good news about Jesus.[4]

3 Quoted in John Blanchard, *The Complete Gathered Gold* (Darlington, UK: Evangelical Press, 2006), 262.

4 Of course, we should remember that from the divine perspective, repentance and faith are gifts that God, in mercy, grants to sinners: Acts 5:31, 11:18; Phil. 1:29; 2 Tim. 2:25.

Repentance and belief are two sides of the same coin of responsibility which are laid upon all who hear the gospel. They are twin graces. As Sinclair Ferguson aptly puts it, they are "marriage partners and never separated."[5] Repentance and faith are intertwined in such a way that when one is mentioned in Scripture, the other is always implied. True repentance cannot occur without faith in Christ's ability to remove and forgive sins, and genuine belief in Christ as Savior necessitates turning away from one's sins altogether. Therefore, according to the Bible, the human response to the gospel is a call for sinners to both repent and believe.

Let's explore these terms more thoroughly. First, *what do I mean by repentance*? In today's world, the concept of repentance needs clarification. In an age like ours, we cannot assume that everyone we speak to knows what we mean when we use such a word. According to the Bible, repentance involves a change of mind and direction in life. It is the work of the Holy Spirit in an individual's life where, out of a true sense of utter helplessness and un-doneness before God and His perfect law, he turns from the error of his ways back to the God whom he has sinned against. Repentance is an actual turning *to* God *from* our rebellion, much like the Thessalonians did. Paul mentions them in the following way: "and how you turned to God from idols to serve the living and true God, and to wait for His Son from heaven, whom He raised from the dead, even Jesus who delivers us from the wrath to come" (1 Thess. 1:9-10).

It is an about-face, characterized by grief over and repudiation of all sin with a desire to forsake it. The Puritans described it as a vomiting of the soul. Repentance means to break off from our past way of life and turn to

---

5 Quoted in Blanchard, *The Complete Gathered Gold*, 201.

Jesus Christ in humble submission and gratitude. Or, as the Westminster Shorter Catechism says in question 87, it is a "saving grace, whereby a sinner, out of a true sense of his sin, and apprehension of the mercy of God in Christ, doth, with grief and hatred of his sin, turn from it unto God, with full purpose of, and endeavor after, new obedience."

Second, *what about belief*? Other words for this are just as helpful to understand its concepts, such as faith and trust. Belief in Christ is not just a head knowledge and assent of who He is and what He's done for us. It is also a complete confidence in and a resting upon who He is and what He's done on our behalf. As Spurgeon helpfully said, "It will not save me to know that Christ is *a* Savior; but it will save me to trust him to be *my* Savior."[6] True saving faith is not a "leap in the dark." Instead, it is based on actual facts grounded in solid evidence concerning Jesus as put forth in the Word of God. This trust in Christ is based on the promises of God's Word: "Whoever believes in Him should not perish but have everlasting life" (John 3:16). And "Believe on the Lord Jesus Christ, and you will be saved, you and your household" (Acts 16:31). Faith is a gift of God which allows an individual to lay hold of Christ and to cast oneself wholly upon Him for mercy and pardon. It is the means or channel through which salvation is received (Eph. 2:8). It is not the human contribution of a sinner seeking salvation, but rather it is the heart's response to and a reception of God's goodness toward us in Jesus Christ the Lord (John 1:12-13; Rom. 5:17, 10:8-11; Col. 2:6). As it has been said, faith has two hands. With one, it stretches out for Christ. With the other, it pushes away all that comes between Christ and the soul. Again, the Westminster Shorter Catechism gets

6 Quoted in Blanchard, *The Complete Gathered Gold*, 203.

the matter right when it says in question 86, "Faith in Jesus Christ as a saving grace, whereby we receive and rest on him alone for salvation as he is offered to us in the gospel."

Scripture consistently commands both repentance and belief.[7] For example, John the Baptist urged the people not only to "Repent" (Matt. 3:2), but he said to them that they should "believe on Him who would come after him, that is, on Christ Jesus" (Acts 19:4). Additionally, in Acts 20:21 we see the apostle Paul going house to house, doing what? The narrative says that he was, "Testifying to Jews, and also to Greeks, repentance toward God (the offended party) and faith toward our Lord Jesus Christ (the only Savior of sinners)." Jesus Himself also preached, "The time is fulfilled, and the kingdom of God is at hand. Repent, and believe in the gospel" (Mark 1:15).

These two commands are inseparable and foundational parts of the gospel message, requiring a response from all who hear it. To be saved, individuals must repent of their sins and believe on Christ alone for life and salvation; these are the hinges upon which the door of salvation freely flies open to them.

Are All Four Parts Necessary?

In practice, it goes without saying, it may not always be possible to communicate all four parts of the gospel. Sometimes, individuals may already be familiar with some aspects of the message, so it won't be necessary to go over all of it again with them. Time constraints may also limit the opportunity to share everything. In some cases, all that will be needed is a clear and concise call to believe on

---

7 See also: John 1:12, 20:31; Acts 3:19, 10:43, 13:38-39, 17:30; 1 Corinthians 1:21, 15:1-2; Galatians 2:16; 1 Timothy 1:16; et al.

Christ. This is seen, for example, with the Philippian jailer (Acts 16:25-34). After he asks Paul and Silas what he must do to be saved, they don't respond to him by saying, "Well, first let me tell you about God, then yourself, then Christ, and so forth." No! Instead, this man was already under deep conviction of sin. He's already in a repentant posture, hence, again, he says *what must I do to be saved?* Further, recall that before this time, Paul had been proclaiming in his streets of Philippi "the way of salvation" (Acts 16:17), so it very well could be that he had already gotten some of the gospel message. Thus, the apostle simply tells him, "Believe on Christ and you will be saved."

In other instances, especially with family members or neighbors, we may take a slower and more thorough approach to this matter. We could walk through each of the four components of the gospel message in a comprehensive fashion while sitting for coffee or tea. Each situation will be different, and each will require sensitivity and Holy Spirit discernment concerning which aspects of the gospel are to be shared. In this chapter, we've covered the central parts of the gospel message. But when you share the gospel with others, don't feel constrained to present it in a canned manner. We are not working through a script. Instead, find out where people are and preach the gospel to them accordingly. If all four parts are needed, then great. If not, prayerfully and humbly share what you can and trust the Lord with the outcome.

The important thing to remember is that the gospel's transformational power lies in *God's work, not your presentation*. Therefore, be faithful and unashamed to share it and leave the results to Him.

For Reflection and Discussion

- What does the word "gospel" mean?
- What are the major fourfold components of the gospel?
- How would you define repentance biblically?
- How would you define faith biblically?

6

The Results of Biblical Evangelism

When Christians evangelize, they are not engaging in some harmless and pleasant pastime. They are engaging in a fearful struggle, the issues of which are eternal.

—Leon Morris

Having considered the message of evangelism, we are now ready to explore its results. What effects should we expect when we share the gospel with others? What type of responses will we get? These questions are crucial to consider. What we believe about this issue will significantly affect our desire, commitment, and willingness to do this blessed work. For instance, if we are convinced that nothing good will come from our witnessing, we will either not do it at all or do so reluctantly and without joy. Conversely, if we naïvely believe that all will go well every time we share the gospel, we will be greatly disappointed and confused to find out that reality often proves otherwise.

Therefore, the issue before us is one of the most important we can consider when it comes to witnessing to the lost. What should our mindset be as we share the good news of Jesus Christ our Lord? How should we anticipate things going?

Among the many passages in the Bible that speak to this subject, few are as helpful as Paul's words in 2 Corinthians 2:12-17. In autobiographical style, Paul recounts to the Corinthians his travels after he left Ephesus (cf. 1:8-10). He describes his journey and how he felt as he waited for Titus's return from Corinth, hoping for an update on the situation in the church. Failing to find Titus in Troas, he continued to Macedonia, where he finally met him and received news about the Corinthians, prompting him to write this letter (2 Cor. 7:5-16). Additionally, Paul is polemical in this passage (v. 17), as he defends his ministry against false teachers who had sought to infiltrate the church and turn the people against him (cf. 11:1-15). Paul writes:

> **Furthermore,** (the word highlighting the beginning of a new section) **when I came to Troas** (Acts 20:6, a city and region in the northwest corner of Asia Minor, modern Turkey) **to preach Christ's gospel** (the words express Paul's primary purpose in going to Troas) **and a door**[1] (a symbol for an opportunity, or an entrance) **was opened** (or quite literally, stood open) **to me by the Lord** (by His doing, His enablement), **I had no rest** (no relief, no peace of mind) **in my spirit** (deep within) **because** (the word giving the reason for the aforementioned thought) **I did not find Titus my brother** (his beloved comrade, traveling companion and ministerial partner and a "true son" in their common faith Titus 1:4); **but** (or so instead) **taking my leave of them, I departed for**

1 Paul uses this metaphor also in 1 Corinthians 16:9; Colossians 4:3. See also Revelation 3:8.

> **Macedonia** (a city in the northern part of Greece). **Now** (or but, the word marking a contrast to Paul's unrest because he did not find Titus at Troas) **thanks** (or praise) **be to God who always** (or at all times) **leads us in triumph** (in victory) **in** (or by means of or through the aid of) **Christ, and through us** (Paul and those who were preaching the gospel of Christ with him and all others after them) **diffuses** (or spreads, and manifest) **the fragrance** (the aroma, the scent) **of His knowledge in every place. For** (or because) **we are to God the fragrance** (like the smell of a pleasant incense) **of Christ among those who are being saved and among those who are perishing. To the one** (those who reject the gospel and are perishing) **we are the aroma of death leading to death, and to the other** (those who embrace it and are being saved) **the aroma of life leading to life. And who is sufficient** (or adequate and competent) **for these things?** (To be able to carry out such a weighty mission with such vast implications joined to it either for eternal salvation or the eternal ruin of souls.) **For we are not, as so many** (the numerous Judaizing false teachers at Corinth), **peddling** (selling for profit like hucksters do) **the word of God; but as of sincerity** (honesty), **but as from God** (as influenced by Him), **we speak in the sight of God** (in His presence, before His face, *Coram Deo*) **in Christ** (in His name, authority and service), (2 Cor. 2:12-17).

Paul's Concern

These verses provide profound insight into what Paul perceived the reception of the gospel would be by those to whom he preached. The matter of preaching the gospel is his central concern as he mentions specifically in verse 12, saying that he went to Troas "to preach Christ's gospel." Paul loved to preach the gospel; it was his great passion and delight. But why was this the case? What fueled his fervor? It was because he understood its transformative power. He knew that when people, by God's grace, believe the message, repent of their sins, and trust in Christ alone to be their Savior, they would be turned "from darkness to light and from the power of Satan to God" (Acts 26:18a). Paul understood that they would then receive the forgiveness of sins and an inheritance among those who are sanctified by faith in Christ (Acts 16:18b).

Yet, despite all of this, Paul was acutely aware of the difficulties that accompanied evangelism. He was not ignorant of the fact that he would suffer many hardships and rejections for Christ's name's sake, just as Jesus told him (Acts 9:15, 16). Even in 2 Corinthians 7:5, in describing his labors, Paul says concerning himself and his companions, "We were troubled on every side. Outside were conflicts, inside were fears." This inner turmoil was compounded by the disappointment of not finding his dear friend Titus in Troas as planned. For reasons unknown, Titus was not there, leaving Paul dispirited. It's no wonder, therefore, that he felt disheartened, and downcast while on the battlefield. From a human perspective, the apostle's circumstances were hard and discouraging.

Paul's Confidence

Despite such discouragement, Paul found solace in reflecting on his God, who is the God of all mercy and comfort (2 Cor. 1:3). As he thought about the Lord's enduring faithfulness to him throughout his ministry, Paul experienced an overwhelming sense of gratitude. Thus, in a spontaneous outpouring of praise, he exclaimed, "Now thanks be to God who always leads us in triumph in Christ" (2 Cor. 2:14). In this moment, we witness Paul's transformation from joylessness to jubilation. As A. T. Robertson, the renowned Greek scholar describes, "Without a word of explanation,

Paul leaps out of the Slough of Despond and sprints like a bird to the heights of joy. He soars aloft like an eagle, with proud scorn of the valley beneath him."[2]

As we consider this passage in the context of biblical evangelism, notice first, Paul is thankful that God *always* leads us in triumph in Christ. The key word here is "always." The point is, as we considered in chapter one, whenever the gospel is proclaimed, our evangelism is successful. Paul doesn't say that God *sometimes* leads us in triumph, or that this is generally so—no. Instead, he says this is true *in every circumstance* and *on all occasions*, even when things seem to be going poorly and trials are mounting. This truth is extremely encouraging and should fortify us as we carry out our task of telling others about Christ. In a world where evangelism is often met with resistance and where our efforts may be mocked or dismissed as too radical or fanatical, it is vital to remember that through our labors God is always leading us in triumph through Jesus Christ our Lord.

But what does Paul mean here by "triumph"? The word "triumph" is a military term, and most scholars agree it would have immediately invoked vivid imagery for the Corinthians, particularly the great spectacle of the ancient world known as the "Roman Triumph,"—a grand procession and special tribute that Rome gave to their conquering generals.

When a Roman general returned from battle victorious, he would at times be honored with a grand parade through the streets of Rome. This parade included the general riding in a golden two-wheeled chariot, pulled by four horses, and surrounded by his soldiers after a great victory. It featured great crowds cheering, music playing, pomp, food, and

---

2 Quoted in William MacDonald, *Believer's Bible Commentary* (Nashville: Thomas Nelson, 1989), 1826.

displays of all sorts, including spoils of the battle such as weapons, jewelry, and other expensive items, as well as the captive enemy soldiers. This procession was also accompanied by the burning of incense along the triumphal route, filling the air with fragrance so that all could smell it.

To the victors, this scent was sweet and joyful. It was a symbol of freedom and life. However, to the captured enemies—the prisoners of war marching in chains—this scent was the bitter smell of defeat and impending death.

What, then, is Paul's point in this word-picture? It is this: God, in Christ, is the great victorious general who leads us, His soldiers, in triumph as we spread His gospel in enemy territory. As we proclaim the gospel, we are like the incense in the triumphal procession, spreading the scent of God's knowledge everywhere we go. Just as a fragrance filled the air in a triumphal procession, the understanding of who God is in the gospel and what He has done for us in Christ also permeates through our faithful witness.

This "fragrance" even reaches to God Himself, for Paul says that we are "to Him" the fragrance of Christ, meaning that our faithful witness is pleasing to God, much like a sweet aroma is satisfying to those who smell it (v. 15a).

Further, Paul says that our witness impacts both "those who are being saved and among those who are perishing" (v. 15b). Here, the apostle divides the entire human race into two categories. He says that to those who are rejecting Christ and the gospel, whose hearts are hardened and who are filled with pride and unbelief—Satan's captives, we are with our message "the aroma of death leading to death." It's not that the message itself means death—no! But that they choose death for themselves by rejecting it of their own volition.

Conversely, to those who are receiving Christ and the gospel, whose hearts are open by the Spirit of God, who feel the guilt of sin and who see the beauty of Jesus as their Savior—God's redeemed captives, we are with our message like a sweet "aroma of life leading to life" (v. 16).

The Twofold Effect of the Gospel

This powerful metaphor highlights the dual impact of biblical evangelism, where the gospel message produces a twin effect. Every time we share the good news of Jesus, those who hear it are scented with the fragrance of the Savior. However, to those who reject the message, what could have been a sweet aroma becomes a stench of death. But, for those who receive the message by faith, the aroma is one of life which leads to eternal life. Notice that these outcomes are opposite—life or death—with no neutral ground. Each time the gospel is proclaimed, this divide emerges: it either becomes a life-giving source for those who receive it or a source of judgment and eternal damnation for those who reject it.

Commenting on this dual effect of the gospel, Calvin is right when he says, "The gospel is preached unto salvation, for that is its real purpose, but only believers share in its salvation. For unbelievers, it is an occasion of condemnation, but it is they who make it so."[3] R. B. Kuiper echoes this with a similar statement, saying, "Man is a free and responsible agent. The unbeliever rejects Christ, not under external compulsion, but of his own choice, yet, under the compulsion of his own nature. His choice is determined by what he is—a totally depraved sinner, at enmity with God."[4]

3 Quoted in Geoffrey B. Wilson, *2 Corinthians,* A Digest of Reformed Comment (Edinburgh: The Banner of Truth, 1973), 37.

4 R. B. Kuiper, *God-Centered Evangelism* (Edinburgh: Banner of Truth, 1966), 233.

This double phenomenon is evident throughout Scripture. For example, Jesus tells us, "He who believes in the Son has everlasting life; and he who does not believe the Son shall not see life, but the wrath of God abides on him" (John 3:36).

Strikingly, this dual effect even occurred at the cross, where our Lord died in the place of sinners. We are told that His work there was life to the thief but death to the other (Luke 23:39-43). Additionally, in the final chapter of Acts, we see the same pattern under Paul's preaching: "So when they had appointed him a day, many came to him at his lodging, to whom he explained and solemnly testified of the kingdom of God, persuading them concerning Jesus from both the Law of Moses and the Prophets, from morning till evening. And some were persuaded by the things which were spoken, and some disbelieved" (Acts 28:23-24). Or, consider what happened when the gospel first reached Iconium:

> Now it happened in Iconium that they went together to the synagogue of the Jews, and so spoke that a great multitude both of the Jews and of the Greeks believed. But the unbelieving Jews stirred up the Gentiles and poisoned their minds against the brethren. Therefore they stayed there a long time, speaking boldly in the Lord, who was bearing witness to the word of His grace, granting signs and wonders to be done by their hands. But the multitude of the city was divided: part sided with the Jews, and part with the apostles (Acts 14:1-4).

This brings us back to my original question: What should our mindset be when we share the gospel? Here it is: we must go out with great confidence, trusting that Jesus will, in fact, save the lost. The gospel *is* "the power of God unto salvation for everyone who believes" (Rom. 1:16), and all who believe on Christ will be saved. This is one of the responses we should eagerly anticipate. We don't know when or who it will happen to, but we know that it has been happening for 2,000 years and will continue to happen until Christ returns—praise be to His Name!

At the same time, we must always remember that some will reject our message; they will think it foolish and consider us fools for proclaiming it. Yet, unless they repent and believe, the message they hear from us will lead to further condemnation for them on the Day of Judgment. This is clear from the teaching of Scripture; therefore the well-known illustration is true: Just as a ray of sunlight can melt butter while at the same time harden clay, so too the gospel we proclaim can melt hearts while at the same time hardening others in their sins.

Should this gospel reality dampen our zeal to reach others with it? God forbid! Instead, it should motivate us to pursue the lost with even greater urgency, while maintaining a sober understanding of the nature of the spiritual battle we are engaged in.

Who Is Sufficient for These Things?

As the apostle contemplated the immense responsibility of preaching the gospel—knowing its far-reaching consequences—he posed a profound question: "Who is sufficient for these things?" (2 Cor. 2:16). This rhetorical question drives home the reality that none of us are adequate for the task of evangelism on our own. We are not inherently capable of bearing the weight of such a calling. However, Paul reassures us that God Himself is the one who makes us sufficient. He underscores this in the next chapter:

"Not that we are sufficient of ourselves to think of anything as being from ourselves, but our sufficiency *is* from God" (2 Cor. 3:5).

Our central passage in view in this chapter teaches us two main truths. First, it emphasizes that *being a witness for Christ is a serious calling*. It's no trivial matter to share the gospel with the lost. From the Bible's perspective, the eternal destinies of men and women hinge on how they respond to the gospel message we bring to them.

Second, it teaches us that *being a witness for Christ is a scented calling*. Paul tells us that "through us" the fragrance of God's knowledge is diffused. Have you considered this lately? God has ordained to reach the unsaved through us who are saved. We are His agents of spreading the gospel as we considered in chapter four. While not everyone will welcome our message, *some will*. This is what makes evangelism a privileged and joyful responsibility. Consequently, we must resist the temptation to believe that nothing good will come from our evangelism, especially when the soil seems hard and unresponsive. At the same time, we should not expect that every effort will be met with a welcome reception and success. This would be unrealistic. This rounded perspective provides us with a biblically grounded, realistic understanding of our task, helping us to persevere with hope and faithfulness even in the face of all sorts of challenges.

What About the Local Church and Discipleship?

This chapter would be incomplete without a conversation about the Christian's commitment to a local church. When someone is converted, the biblical pattern is that their new-found faith will result in them being connected to a biblically sound, Christ-centered, gospel-preaching church.

Unfortunately, many today have a truncated view of evangelism, seeing it solely as a means of getting people saved and nothing more. While we should greatly desire and fervently pray for the salvation of souls, this is only part of the picture. Scripture also teaches that after sinners are saved by God's grace, they will then grow into mature disciples who will live the whole of their lives for His glory and honor (1 Cor. 10:31; Eph. 4:14-15; 2 Pet. 3:18).[5] Salvation is only the beginning of a saved life that should continue in the context of a biblical local church. If we are only interested in seeing converts without ensuring their growth and instruction in the faith, we fall short of the biblical mandate. Again, Kuiper wisely notes: "The truth of the matter is that church membership is a normal and necessary consequence [or result] of salvation."[6]

This is particularly evident in the Great Commission, as recorded in Matthew's gospel. Here, as we discussed in chapter two, Jesus appears to His disciples as the risen King. He is no longer the Man of Sorrows, but the one who has been given "all authority in heaven and on earth" (Matt. 28:18). In view of this authority, Jesus commissioned His disciples to make disciples, baptize them, and teach them (Matt. 28:19-20). But the question is, what is the context in which these commands are to be carried out? Are new

5 Discipleship is about learning from and following hard after Jesus in every area of our lives, all the days of our lives, according to His Word and by the power of the Holy Spirit. A helpful resource in this regard is *Radical Discipleship: Uncompromising Conviction in a Hostile World* by Hensworth W. C. Jonas (Grand Rapids: Reformation Heritage Books, 2024).

6 R. B. Kuiper, *God-Centered Evangelism*, 111.

converts expected to baptize themselves and then grow in isolation, perhaps by watching YouTube sermons? Of course not! Rather, these commands are to be fulfilled within the framework of a local church, which is God's appointed agent for carrying out the Great Commission and nurturing believers in their faith.

But how do we know this was the understanding of the early apostles who first heard our Lord's words? Acts 2 makes the point clear. After the Holy Spirit descended on the apostles at Pentecost, Peter preaches and 3,000 souls were saved (Acts 2:1-4, 14-21). What happened next? Does Peter just dismiss the crowds, telling them to go on their merry way? No, rather the passage tells us that those who were saved were baptized and added to the local community of believers: "And with many other words he testified and exhorted them, saying, 'Be saved from this perverse generation.' Then those who gladly received his word were baptized; and that day about three thousand souls were added to them. And they continued steadfastly in the apostles' doctrine and fellowship, in the breaking of bread, and in prayers" (Acts 2:40-42). A few verses later we are told that "the Lord added to the church daily those who were being saved" (Acts 2:47).

This shows us that biblical evangelism is never meant to be separated from the context of a local church, as seen in the case of the church in Jerusalem. Can people be saved without joining a local church? Can they be discipled apart from a local church? Yes. But in the main, such a practice is unbiblical and will lead to unhealthy aberrations, discouragements, and disappointments in the life of the believer. This is why, even when Paul was converted on the road to Damascus (Acts 9:1-9), one of the first things he did after receiving his sight was attempt to join the church in Jerusalem (Acts 9:26). The apostle had just had an encounter with the risen Lord Jesus Christ the King of glory. Therefore, if anyone had an excuse not to join a local church, it was him! However, he does the exact opposite. He was eager to commit himself to a local body of believers, for he understood that after people were saved, they were to be formally part of Jesus' body, as expressed in a local congregation.

Further, even though Christ directly commissioned the apostle to be His chosen vessel in order to bear his name before Gentiles, kings, and the children of Israel (Acts 9:15), he did not launch out on his own to the mission field. Instead, after being involved in the church in Antioch for some time, he was sent out by the church there, underscoring the crucial role of the local church in every aspect of the Christian's life, mission and ministry (Acts 13:1-3).

In summary, according to the New Testament, a Christian who is disconnected from formal membership in a local church is very much out of step with biblical Christianity. This is an anomaly that must be corrected at once. Therefore, when people respond in faith to the gospel, afterwards they need to be baptized, taught, and discipled within the context of a church under the oversight of a godly, qualified, gospel-focused, Christ-centered leadership. Evangelism is intended to lead to integration into the life of the local church, where Christians can learn, grow together, and "with one mind and one mouth glorify the God and Father of our Lord Jesus Christ" (Rom. 15:6).

For Reflection and Discussion

- What results should we expect when we share the gospel with others?
- What key passages support this truth?
- Should this biblical truth stifle or stimulate our evangelistic zeal? Or maybe it should create another disposition in us?
- Concerning the results of biblical evangelism, what part should the local church play in this process?

7

The Power for Biblical Evangelism

But you shall receive power when the Holy Spirit has come upon you; and you shall be witnesses to Me in Jerusalem, and in all Judea and Samaria, and to the end of the earth.

—Jesus (Acts 1:8)

In one of his lively lectures to his students at his pastoral college, Charles Haddon Spurgeon passionately shared his thoughts on the Holy Spirit, saying:

> "I believe in the Holy Ghost." Having pronounced that sentence as a matter of creed, I hope we can also repeat it as a devout soliloquy forced to our lips by personal experience. To us the presence and work of the Holy Spirit are the ground of our confidence as to the wisdom and hopefulness of our life work. If we had *not* believed in the Holy Ghost we should have laid down our ministry long ere this, for "who is sufficient for these things?" Our hope of success, and our strength for

> continuing the service, lie in our belief that the Spirit of the Lord rests upon us.[1]

For Spurgeon, these weren't just nice-sounding words—they were deeply held convictions. In fact, it is said that every time he stepped into the pulpit, he silently repeated to himself, "I believe in the Holy Spirit, I believe in the Holy Spirit, I believe in the Holy Spirit." Throughout his ministry, Spurgeon consistently emphasized his reliance on the person and power of the Holy Spirit for the proclamation of the gospel.

As Christians, we should affirm with Spurgeon, "I *believe* in the Holy Spirit." However, when it comes to the work of evangelism, I wonder how many of us feel the urgency to cry out to the Lord, saying, "I *need* the Holy Spirit!" But who is the Holy Spirit, and why do we desperately need Him and His power for every aspect of our outreach? Why must we have Him and His strength for this most strategic effort? As we approach the final chapter of this book, these are the vital questions we will look at.

The Holy Spirit's Person[2]

In answering the question of who is the Holy Spirit, we turn to the Word of God. The Scriptures are abundantly plain regarding this matter. The Bible tells us that the Holy Spirit is the eternal third person of the blessed Trinity (Matt. 28:19). The Holy Spirit is God (Acts 5:3-4), of the same essence as and equal to the Father and the Son (Matt. 3:16-17; 1 Cor. 12:4-6;

---

1 C. H. Spurgeon, *Lectures To My Students*, (Grand Rapids: Zondervan, 1973), 185.

2 A portion of the material in this chapter comes from a piece I wrote on *The Holy Spirit and the Preacher of God*, which has appeared in various publications.

2 Cor. 13:14; Eph. 4:4-6; 1 John 5:7), yet all three are distinct (Luke 1:35, 3:21, 22, 12:10; John 16:7-15; 1 Cor. 12:4-6; Rev. 1:4-5), while being one God (Deut. 6:4; 1 Cor. 8:6).

Consider first, that the Holy Spirit is a *person.*[3] Some distinct personal characteristics of the Holy Spirit are: His ability to teach (Neh. 9:20; Luke 12:12; John 14:26; 1 John 2:27), testify (John 15:26), convict (John 16:8), lead (Rom. 8:14; Acts 8:29, 13:2, 16:6-7; 2 Pet. 1:21), seal (Eph. 1:13-14, 4:30), appoint (Acts 13:2), equip (1 Cor. 12:4-10; Rom. 12:4-13), intercede (Rom. 8:26-27), search (1 Cor. 2:10-11), and grieve (Isa. 63:10; Eph. 4:30). Also, the Holy Spirit can be lied to and insulted (Acts 5:3; Heb. 10:29).

Consider second, that the Holy Spirit is a *divine person.*[4] The Holy Spirit is called God (Acts 5:4; 2 Cor. 3:17), and divine attributes are ascribed to Him, such as omnipresence (Ps. 139:7-10; 2 Cor. 3:17), omniscience (Isa. 40:13-14; John 14:26; 1 Cor. 2:10-11), omnipotence (Luke 1:35; Rom. 9:11, 15:19), eternality (Heb. 9:14), and creativity (Gen. 1:2; Job 26:13, 33:4; Ps. 104:30). Additionally, the Holy Spirit regenerates (John 3:5-6, 6:63; Titus 3:5), sanctifies (2 Thess. 2:13), and glorifies (John 16:14; Rom. 8:11). He also inspired the Word of God (2 Pet. 1:20-21) and can be blasphemed (Mark 3:29).

After seeing the scriptural witness to the personality and divine being of the Holy Spirit, isn't it clear that because of who He is, He is absolutely essential to our mission of reaching the lost? Let us not miss the crucial point: just as we cannot do any gospel good without the aid of God the Father or Christ the Son, the same is true of the Holy Spirit.

---

3 The Holy Spirit is not a vague, impersonal force. This is the teaching of the Jehovah's Witness organization.

4 See also 2LBCF 2.3.

Without Him, we cannot accomplish anything of lasting spiritual value. Without Him, even our best efforts will prove useless, for as Jesus said in John 6:63, "It is the Spirit who gives life; the flesh profits nothing."

Think about what we're up against every time we engage the lost with the gospel. The hearts of unsaved people are "full of evil and madness" (Eccles. 9:3) and are "deceitful above all things and desperately wicked" (Jer. 17:9). They themselves are "slaves of sin" (Rom. 6:20), and held captive to their false beliefs, bound and under "the spiritual sway of the wicked one" (1 John 5:19). This is why evangelism requires more than mere words—it demands the power of the Holy Spirit to back those words and to break through these barriers. We need the Spirit to give us spiritual boldness to speak truth into this dark and rebellious world. We need spiritual empowerment to effectively proclaim Christ to this evil and adulterous generation. But let's face it—we don't have the power to effectively convince men of their sins and their need to turn to Christ. We don't have the ability to make them see the glories of our wonderful Savior. So, what is the answer?

The Holy Spirit's Ministry

Now that we've talked about who the Holy Spirit is according to Scripture, let's consider what His ministry is and how it applies to us as we seek to reach the lost with the gospel. The Holy Spirit's role is multifaceted, and it touches on several key areas such as *illumination*—the opening of the heart and mind to receive and grasp divinely revealed scriptural truth (1 Cor. 2:14-16; Eph. 1:17-18); *fruit-bearing*—the character traits and attitudes of God's true children that the Holy Spirit produces in them

(Gal. 5:22-23);[5] and *filling*—the repeated experience of the believer whereby they are enabled to accomplish some particular task or service for God (Exod. 31:3; Acts 4:8, 31, 7:55; Eph. 5:18). That said, our specific focus here will be on the power of the Spirit to the Christian.

But What Is This Power?

Let me be clear: *the power to evangelize the lost is not something separate from the Holy Spirit Himself—it is a direct, heightened expression of His presence and work in and upon us as believers.* Every Christian receives the gift of the Holy Spirit at the moment of conversion once for all time. Despite what some teach today, this isn't a second blessing or something we chase after. Rather, as Paul says in Ephesians 1:13, "In Him (Jesus) you also trusted, after you heard the word of truth, the gospel of your salvation; in whom also, having believed, you were sealed with the Holy Spirit of promise."[6]

Because of this fact, every Christian is already indwelt and empowered for the work of evangelism. Indeed, fresh infillings of the Holy Spirit can newly empower us for impactful evangelism (Acts 4:8, 31), but the fact remains that because He permanently dwells within us, we now have the ability to effectively proclaim Christ to the lost. His presence in us enables us to rise above our human limitations. As John MacArthur correctly observes, "Every Christian is packed with the power from the Holy Spirit. So if you ever feel you are lacking in power, remember God's efficient provision for you—His Holy Spirit who already dwells within you."[7]

---

5 For a detailed consideration of each fruit of the Spirit, I refer the reader to my series on this subject on sermonaudio.com.

6 See also John 7:37-39; Acts 11:15-17; Galatians 3:2.

7 John MacArthur, *The Ministry of the Holy Spirit*, Spotlight on Scripture (Sun Valley: Grace to You), 9.

The Bible shows that "Spirit" and "power" regularly go together. Several passages bear this out:

> The Spirit of the Lord shall rest upon Him, the Spirit of wisdom and understanding, the Spirit of counsel and might, the Spirit of knowledge and of the fear of the Lord. (Isa. 11:2)
>
> But truly I am full of power by the Spirit of the Lord, and of justice and might, to declare to Jacob his transgression and to Israel his sin. (Micah 3:8)
>
> … and declared to be the Son of God with power according to the Spirit of holiness, by the resurrection from the dead. (Rom. 1:4)
>
> Now may the God of hope fill you with all joy and peace in believing, that you may abound in hope by the power of the Holy Spirit. (Rom. 15:13)
>
> … in mighty signs and wonders, by the power of the Spirit of God, so that from Jerusalem and round about to Illyricum I have fully preached Christ. (Rom. 15:19)
>
> For God has not given us a Spirit of fear, but of power and of love and of a sound mind. (2 Tim. 1:7)[8]

Moreover, in Scripture, the Holy Spirit is said to empower His people for various works of service. Several scriptural examples illustrate this:

> The Spirit of the Lord came upon him, and he judged Israel. (Judg. 3:10)
>
> But the Spirit of the Lord came upon Gideon; then he blew the trumpet, and the Abiezrites gathered behind him. (Judg. 6:34)

---

8 I am aware of the debate regarding the word "spirit" in this passage. At present, I believe that the word has reference to the Holy Spirit. For further support of this view, please see William Hendriksen and Simon J. Kistemaker, *New Testament Commentary, Thessalonians, the Pastorals and Hebrews* (Grand Rapids: Baker Book House, 1995), 228-29.

> Then the Spirit of the LORD came upon Jephthah, and he passed through Gilead and Manasseh, and passed through Mizpah of Gilead; and from Mizpah of Gilead he advanced toward the people of Ammon. (Judg. 11:29)

> Then Samuel took the horn of oil and anointed him in the midst of his brothers; and the Spirit of the LORD came upon David from that day forward. (1 Sam. 16:13)

Where Else Is This Topic Addressed?

When we think about this specific aspect of power for the believer in relation to the Holy Spirit and evangelism, let's start with Luke 24. As Jesus prepares His disciples for the extraordinary task of global evangelism, He makes it clear that the power of the Holy Spirit is crucial and necessary for their mission.

After instructing them in Luke 24:47 that "repentance and remission of sins should be preached in His name to all nations, beginning at Jerusalem" and that they were witnesses of these things" (v. 48)—meaning, "not only witnesses of the events surrounding the work of Christ but also of the commission itself to spread the gospel"[9]—Jesus says to them next, "Behold, I send you *the Promise of my Father upon you, but tarry in the city of Jerusalem until you are endued (clothed) with power from on high*" (v. 49). But what is this Promise? Or rather *Who* is this Promise?

The Promise is the Holy Spirit Himself. He is the one they would receive on the day of Pentecost, as described in Acts 2 and predicted in Joel 2:28. But why did they need the Holy Spirit and His power? It's simple: they needed Him to carry out the tremendous evangelistic commission Jesus gave them. This was no small task. In fact, in many ways, it

9 David Guzik, *Commentary on the Gospel of Luke*, Enduring Word Commentary Series (Goleta, CA: Enduring Word, 2019), 422.

was a daunting one, especially since the disciples would face much persecution as they preached Christ to the crowds. So, in obedience to the Lord, the disciples stayed in the city of Jerusalem, waiting for the Promise and the power.

This brings us second to Acts 1:4-8. After Jesus reminds them of this Promise in verses four and five, the disciples asked Him, "Lord, will you at this time restore the kingdom of God?" (v. 6). Unfortunately, this question seems to show that the disciples had slipped back into their old way of thinking, confusing the promise and power of the Father with an earthly restoration of a political, national kingdom.

Jesus gently corrects their confusion by saying, "It is not for you to know the times or seasons which the Father has put in His own authority" (v. 7). In other words, He tells them to focus on the task at hand—the mission they've been given. Then, in strong contrast to their question about political power, Jesus says, "But you shall receive power when (at that moment) the Holy Spirit has come upon you and (the result) you shall be witnesses to me in Jerusalem and in Judea and Samaria, and to the end of the earth" (v. 8).

With this, our Lord encourages His followers for the work at hand, letting them know that the coming of the Holy Spirit upon them would give them the spiritual capability they need in order to be courageous witnesses for Him. The Spirit's empowerment would help them speak God's truth with significant effect. We see this in action for example, when after the Apostle Peter was filled with the Spirit (Acts 2:4), he preached the gospel to the lost on Pentecost and "three thousand souls" were saved (Acts 2:41). Far beyond his natural abilities, Peter was emboldened by the Spirit to preach Christ most extraordinarily, leading to the salvation of a great multitude, and this as he spoke "by the Holy Spirit sent from heaven" (1 Pet. 1:12).

It's worth noting that Jesus Himself also knew the power of the Holy Spirit upon His earthly ministry to accomplish all that His Father had commissioned Him to do. Consequently, it makes perfect sense that He would speak to His followers about this subject. Before beginning His public ministry, we're told that after His temptation, He "*returned in the power of the Spirit to Galilee*" (Luke 4:14).[10] Later in that same chapter of Luke, we're told that after He read from Isaiah, He said, "*The Spirit of the Lord is upon Me, because He has anointed Me to preach the gospel to the poor*" (Luke 4:18). In Matthew's gospel the power of the Holy Spirit was evident upon His labors so He said, "But if I cast out demons *by the Spirit of God*, surely the kingdom of God has come upon you" (Matt. 12:28). And then in Acts 10:38, Peter says, "How God anointed Jesus of Nazareth *with the Holy Spirit and with power*."

So, here's the key question: if Jesus needed the Spirit and His power for His labors, how much more do we? If the Son of God needed this, what about us? The answer is obvious! And the good news is, just as God gave the Holy Spirit to Christ and promised His Spirit and power to the early disciples, He gives the same to us, His people, today.

Bible commentator William McDonald helpfully remarks on this topic when he says,

> This power is the grand indispensable of Christian witness. A man may be highly talented, intensively trained, and widely experienced, but without spiritual power he is ineffective. On the other hand, a man may be uneducated, unattractive, and unrefined, yet let him be endued with the power of the

10 See also Isaiah 42:1, 61:1-2; Matthew 12:28; Luke 4:1, 18-21.

> Holy Spirit and the world will turn out to see him burn for God. The fearful disciples needed powerful witnessing, holy boldness for preaching the gospel. They would receive this power when the Holy Spirit came upon them.[11]

Consider, third, 1 Corinthians 2. After establishing in the previous chapter that it "pleased God through the foolishness of the message preached to save those who believe" (1:21), Paul contrasts his ministry with that of the popular philosophers and Greco-Roman rhetoricians of his time, saying, "And my speech and my preaching were not with persuasive words of human wisdom, but in demonstration of the Spirit and of power" (2:4).

Here, in this verse, the apostle uses the strong Greek adversative (*alla*) translated as "but" to clearly distinguish what his preaching was and was not. Negatively, it was not "with persuasive words of human wisdom," but positively, it was "in demonstration of the Spirit and of power." F. W. Grosheide comments, "This does not mean that Paul in his preaching displayed spirit and power, but rather that the Holy Spirit and the power of God (1:18, 24) manifested themselves in his preaching."[12]

What Paul is saying to the Corinthians is: the reason you came to faith in Christ wasn't because of my cleverness of speech or any well-polished oratory skills that I had. But rather, it was because, when I preached, the Holy Spirit's power worked in and through me. David E. Garland notes,

> Paul did not win them over as the perfect master of the art of oratory. Instead, they were confronted with divine proof,

11 William McDonald, *Believers Bible Commentary*, 1579.

12 F.W. Grosheide, *Commentary on the First Epistle to the Corinthians* (Grand Rapids: Wm. B. Eerdmans Publishing, 1953), 61.

> "the demonstration of the Spirit and Power." What is clear is that Paul attributes the Corinthians' conversion to the powerful intervention of the Spirit ...The proof of this power is not the audience's round of applause for the preacher's oratorical art but their changed lives and the formation of a new community.[13]

Once again, in this passage, the matters of Spirit and power are linked together. This shows us that Paul clearly understood that the Holy Spirit and His power were vital in his ministry to produce results in his hearers. The same must be true for us as we witness to the lost since the Holy Spirit is the most significant source of power for evangelism. People turning from their sins and coming to Christ for salvation are not things we can produce in them. They are not the results of human ingenuity or rhetorical fanfare but exclusively the Holy Spirit's persuasion. When we witness to others, we often feel weak and powerless for the task at hand. So the questions arise: has the Lord made any provision for us in this regard? Is there any help available to us? The answer is yes! And that help is "power from on high" available to us in the Holy Spirit. This is a truth we must remind ourselves of again and again because we sometimes forget it and are quick to trust in everything but the Holy Spirit to equip us for the work of evangelism. Too often, we rely on the flesh. We trust in programs and pageantry, but what we need most of all is omnipotent power—which is in God's omnipotent Spirit.

Consider fourth and finally, 1 Thessalonians 1:5. After stating that the Thessalonians were *an energetic church* (vv. 1-3) and noting in verse 4, that they were also *an*

13 David E. Garland, *1 Corinthians* (Grand Rapids: Baker Book House, 2003), 86-87.

elect church—"knowing, beloved brethren, your election by God,"—Paul then presents the external proof of their election in verse 5, "*For our gospel did not come to you in word only, but also in power and in the Holy Spirit and in much assurance as you know what kind of men we were among you for your sakes.*" In this verse, the apostle highlights two aspects of his preaching to the Thessalonians. First, he says it came to them in human words. In other words, the gospel was not communicated to them by some means other than by a human being, which in this case was mainly Paul himself. Second, he emphasizes that his gospel did not come to them in human words only, "but also in power and in the Holy Spirit."

Again, he uses the strong Greek adversative (*alla*) "but" to stress a point of sharp contrast. Yes, these believers should be assured of their election by God because they received God's Word, but they also needed to understand that the gospel message they believed was not merely received because of the speaking ability of a man. Instead, it was believed because when Paul preached, he did so in the power of the Holy Spirit, so that with God's blessings, it resulted in them receiving the gospel message in "much assurance." Paul makes it clear that the preaching of a mere man, unaccompanied by the Spirit's dynamic power, will be ineffective in the lives of those who hear it. It will not bring regeneration (Titus 3:5) or the conviction of sin (John 16:8), which only the Holy Spirit can bring.

What all this shows us is that if we want our gospel outreach to make a real impact, we absolutely need the Holy Spirit's help. For our evangelizing to be effective, His power must be our portion. This is the fact of the matter, because, once again, in and of ourselves, we are utterly incapable of producing any good or lasting change in the lives of those who hear us. Therefore, the Holy Spirit's ministry to us is crucial if sinners are to be saved. Spurgeon nicely sums up the matter:

> If there is to be a divine result from God's Word, the Holy Ghost must go forth with it. As surely as God went before the children of Israel when He divided the Red Sea, as surely as He led them through the wilderness by the pillar of cloud and fire, so surely must the Lord's powerful presence go with His word if there is to be any blessing from it.[14]

How Can We Know More of the Holy Spirit's Ministry?

Now that we've explored who the Holy Spirit is and some key aspects of His work in relationship to the believer, the final question that needs to be asked is, "How can we experience more of His ministry?" We know we need the Holy Spirit's ministry, but how we can know more of it upon us is not always so plain. Throughout church history, many have tried to answer this question, often with misconceptions.[15] To avoid these errors, we must ground our understanding and practices firmly on Scripture. If we want to know more of the Holy Spirit's work in our lives, there are a few indispensable matters we should always keep in mind. Let me break them down with three main points:

First, negatively, if we are to know more of the Holy Spirit's ministry resting upon us for evangelism, then we must be sure that we are not grieving Him. Ephesians 4:30 exhorts us,

14 C. H. Spurgeon, *An All Around Ministry* (Edinburgh: Banner Of Truth Trust, 1960), 339.

15 Here I am thinking about such groups as the Montanist (Second Century), Anabaptist (Fifteenth Century), Shakers (Seventeenth Century) and the Wesleyans Methodist (Eighteenth Century) who sought a "second blessing" experience from God.

"And do not grieve the Holy Spirit of God, by which you were sealed for the day of redemption." The fact that the Holy Spirit can be grieved proves again our initial assertion that He is a person. The word "grieve" here means to cause pain, sorrow, and mourning. The context of verses 25-29 and verse 31 bears out for us how we might grieve the Holy Spirit, namely by lying, having unrighteous anger, stealing, speaking corrupt words, harboring bitterness, wrath, malice, etc. These sins and others, including pride, lust, dishonesty, and all uncleanness, must grieve Him as well. We must remember that the Spirit is the *Holy* Spirit and He will not be pleased where unconfessed and unrepented sin exists. In short, any unresolved moral or ethical controversy between us and God, or between us and others, will hinder our communion with the Holy Spirit and prevent His ministry from being powerfully operative in our lives and upon our labors.

Second, if we are to know more of the Holy Spirit's ministry resting upon us for evangelism, then we must be sure that we are not quenching Him. In 1 Thessalonians 5:19 we read, "Do not quench the Spirit." The term "quench" means, "to put out," as one puts out a fire.[16] While, of course, we cannot "quench" the Spirit so as to completely "quench Him out"—because as we have seen, He is God—we can nonetheless quench Him in the sense of hindering or stifling His person and ministry in our lives.

A helpful way to understand what the apostle is here commanding us not to do is to translate the verse as "Do not pour water on the Holy Spirit's fire." As in the passage

16 Cleon L. Roger Jr. and Cleon L. Rogers III, *The New Linguistic and Exegetical Key to the Greek New Testament* (Grand Rapids: Zondervan, 1998), 481.

considered in Ephesians, no doubt, sin in our lives would surely be one way of quenching the Spirit's ministry amongst us. Additionally, it might be said that the quenching of the Spirit can occur when we do not recall who He is and how much we desperately need Him in our lives and our gospel labors.

Perhaps as various commentators have noted, we have here at Thessalonica an opposite problem than that of Corinth. In Corinth, the people were *overemphasizing* the Spirit; at Thessalonica, they were *underemphasizing* Him. In Corinth, Paul had to restrain excesses; in Thessalonica, he had to forbid repression.

Third, then, positively, if we are to know more of the Holy Spirit's ministry resting upon us for evangelism, we must be sure that we are regularly asking God for fresh measures of the Holy Spirit Himself. Since the Holy Spirit has multiple ministries in our lives, including giving us power from on high, we must be sure that we frequently ask God for fresh measures of Him. In Luke 11:13, Jesus says, "If you then, being evil know how to give good gifts to your children, how much more will your heavenly Father give the Holy Spirit to those who ask Him!" Here our Lord argues from the lesser to the greater to prove a point: if we, despite all of our sins and flaws, know how to give good gifts to our children, "how much more" will our perfect, sinless heavenly Father give the Holy Spirit to those who ask.

The incentive to ask for the Holy Spirit is embedded in the center of Jesus' words. He compares us, who "are evil," with God, who is not, and then says: ask, and He will give the Holy Spirit to us. Based on this promise, the continual giving and supply of the Holy Spirit is for those who ask.

Therefore, this is what we must do. We must ask! We must continue to ask! We must never stop asking!

We Need the Holy Spirit!

How can we possibly tackle the incredible task of evangelizing the lost? Where do we find the power, strength, and ability in order to face this most challenging task? Thankfully, the answer does not lie within ourselves. Instead, the answer is found in the Holy Spirit Himself.

If we genuinely believe this, by God's grace, we will live uprightly as His people, understanding the essential connection between how we live and the Holy Spirit's richest blessings upon us. Further, if we genuinely believe this, we will be quick to cry out to God regularly whenever we're about to witness to someone, saying, "Oh Lord, empower me afresh with the Spirit so that I may speak as I ought to speak" (cf. Col. 4:4). Dear reader, if you embrace these perspectives, you will find that the power for evangelistic service will be yours. By doing so, you will find yourself significantly "strengthened with might through His Spirit in the inner man" (Eph. 3:16).

For Reflection and Discussion

- Who is the Holy Spirit according to the Bible?
- Why do we need His power for the work of evangelism?
- What is His power, and what Scriptures connect Him to power?
- How can we know more of the Holy Spirit's ministry in our lives for the work of evangelism?

Conclusion

And He said to them, "Go into all the world and preach the gospel to every creature."

—Mark 16:15

Our Lord's Great Commission is indeed a *great commission.* It is a command of profound significance, as it concerns the never-dying souls of lost individuals who are currently on the broad road that "leads to destruction" (Matt. 7:13). Through our obedience to this charge, our Lord transforms sinners into saints, rebels into the righteous, and the lost into devout lovers of Himself. The work of sharing the gospel with the unsaved as a means of God bringing about these transformations is both mighty and daunting. We face countless challenges as Christians, and the potential for things to go amiss is real. It is for this reason that I have written this book. This is why I have labored—to provide you with a solid foundation for the work ahead. In this endeavor, I have sought to construct a biblical and systematic approach to our topic, guiding you step-by-step through this vital subject. I have aimed to impress upon you the weight and urgency of this most sacred matter and to equip you for it. Therefore, I pray that this material will serve as a powerful springboard to enable and encourage you to proclaim boldly, yet lovingly and gracefully, our glorious Savior to the unsaved around you. May He Himself be pleased to use this work to this great end—for His supreme glory, your spiritual benefit, and the strategic rescue and restoration of many. Amen.

Further Reading

Joel R. Beeke, *Puritan Evangelism* (Grand Rapids: Reformation Heritage Books, 1999)

Thomas Boston, *The Art of Man-Fishing* (Fearn: Christian Heritage, 2012)

Walter J. Chantry, *Today's Gospel: Authentic or Synthetic?* (Edinburgh: Banner of Truth, 1970)

Ryan Denton, *Ten Modern Evangelism Myths: A Modern Corrective* (Grand Rapids: Reformation Heritage Books, 2021)

J. I. Packer, *Evangelism & the Sovereignty of God* (Lisle: InterVarsity Press, 2010)

Ernest C. Reisinger, *Today's Evangelism: Its Message and Methods* (Phillipsburg: P&R Publishing, 1982)

Charles Spurgeon, *The Soul Winner* (Fearn: Christian Heritage, 1992)

Jeremy Walker, T*he Brokenhearted Evangelist* (Grand Rapids: Reformation Heritage Books, 2012)

Paul Washer, *The Gospel's Power & Message* (Grand Rapids: Reformation Heritage Books, 2012)

Christian Focus Publications

Our mission statement

Staying Faithful

In dependence upon God we seek to impact the world through literature faithful to His infallible Word, the Bible. Our aim is to ensure that the Lord Jesus Christ is presented as the only hope to obtain forgiveness of sin, live a useful life and look forward to heaven with Him.

Our Books are published in four imprints:

CHRISTIAN FOCUS

Popular works including biographies, commentaries, basic doctrine and Christian living.

MENTOR

Books written at a level suitable for Bible College and seminary students, pastors, and other serious readers. The imprint includes commentaries, doctrinal studies, examination of current issues and church history.

CHRISTIAN HERITAGE

Books representing some of the best material from the rich heritage of the church.

CF4KIDS

Children's books for quality Bible teaching and for all age groups: Sunday school curriculum, puzzle and activity books; personal and family devotional titles, biographies and inspirational stories – because you are never too young to know Jesus!

Christian Focus Publications Ltd,
Geanies House, Fearn, Ross-shire,
IV20 1TW, Scotland, United Kingdom.
www.christianfocus.com